WHISKY

WHISKY

By

AENEAS MACDONALD

EDINBURGH

CANONGATE BOOKS

FIRST PUBLISHED IN MCMXXX
BY THE PORPOISE PRESS
133A GEORGE STREET, EDINBURGH

REPUBLISHED IN GREAT BRITAIN IN MMVI
BY CANONGATE BOOKS LTD
14 HIGH STREET, EDINBURGH

I

BRITISH LIBRARY CATALOGUING-IN-PUBLICATION DATA
A CATALOGUE RECORD FOR THIS BOOK IS AVAILABLE
ON REQUEST FROM THE BRITISH LIBRARY

1 84195 857 3 (10-DIGIT ISBN)
978 1 84195 857 6 (13-DIGIT ISBN)

PRINTED AND BOUND IN GERMANY BY
GGP MEDIA GMBH, POESSNECK

Foreword

CHARLES MACLEAN

If I could only take one whisky book to a desert island, it would be Aeneas MacDonald's *Whisky*.

It is a shining gem of a book – polemic, passionate, provocative, poetic; romantic (nothing wrong with that); beautifully written; so amusing in places that I laugh out loud, yet so well-informed that I long suspected its author to have been a distiller or an exciseman.

Many are the bar-room conversations I have had with other whisky scholars about the identity of Aeneas MacDonald. Why did so obviously talented a writer publish no more? Why does his name not appear in the broader context of 'The Scottish Literary Revival', in which The Porpoise Press, his publisher, played such a key role? It seemed to us that 'Aeneas MacDonald' must be a pseudonym. Then who was he?

The Porpoise Press also published Neil M. Gunn, author of *Whisky and Scotland* (1935) and himself an exciseman. I wondered for a long time whether Gunn and Macdonald were the same person – the latter matches the former for poetry and insider-information about the whisky trade. For his humour and elegance, I also speculated whether 'Aeneas MacDonald' might not be Archie G. MacDonnell, author of that priceless work, *England, Their England* (1933).

With diligent and imaginative research, Ian Buxton has now solved the mystery once and for all – and the truth is not disappointing, as you will discover when you read his introduction. Far from it: with this publication, Mr Buxton has firmly installed the real 'Aeneas Macdonald' in the pantheon of Scottish writers of the twentieth century.

More than this, he has brought a wonderful, but now rare, book to the attention of a new generation of readers. He deserves our thanks and congratulations, as does his publisher, Canongate – the latter-day Porpoise Press!

Charles MacLean, 2006

Aeneas MacDonald's Whisky – An appreciation

IAN BUXTON

'Why should I read this book? It's more than seventy-five years old . . .'

It's not an unreasonable question: by a conservative estimate there are now at least two hundred books about, or mainly about, whisky. The shelves overflow with titles, and new works are added at an ever-increasing pace – a dozen or more annually.

Yet, despite the fact that the first written record of Scotch whisky is found as long ago as 1494 and distilling is even described in the sixth century by the Welsh bard Taliesin, by some extraordinary omission no one thought it of sufficient interest or importance to write from the point of view of the drinker, the consumer, the *humble lover of Scotch*, until 1930.

For this alone, Aeneas MacDonald deserves your time, your attention and your respect. With this slim volume, he began whisky's renaissance. MacDonald still speaks to us today: on how, when and why to drink whisky; on why whisky – especially good whisky – matters; even on what it means to be Scottish he is a sure and certain guide. And, at its simplest, this is also a damn good read: with glass and bottle at your side, you will look with new enjoyment on your dram and dawning respect at a text that, yes, is more than seventy-five years old – but remains as fresh as a new-drawn cask sample: bright, sparkling and full of rich promise.

In fact, given today's near obsessive interest in the subject, and the importance of whisky to the national psyche, identity and economy, it seems quite remarkable that Scotland should have waited so long for MacDonald.

As he says, 'whisky-drinkers are not yet mere soakers, in spite of the scant attention paid to their enlightenment by the trade' yet, until his work, the industry was a closed book. Thus, every subsequent writer on whisky is in his debt, and every considered drinker.

We may list the faults in MacDonald (a fondness for doggerel not least), but his prose never once lacks for poetry. A love of whisky permeates his soul. Time is transcended by passages of passionate, lyrical beauty and we are transfixed by the soaring spirit and graceful imagination of a true acolyte. *Whisky* is simply a joy to read.

But we live in an age of league tables and cost-benefit

analysis, where passion is distrusted and spreadsheets thought to contain the very secrets of our universe. Surely, in a world where an inventory of capacities passes for an initiation into the sacred mysteries of the still, MacDonald has nothing to teach us. What, you may ask, can I *learn* from this book?

Well, if utility is all you seek there is value still in these pages. Here, for example, we will find the first practical instruction in nosing and tasting whisky, MacDonald's guidelines for which, even including the selection of glassware, are reliable to this day.

More importantly, he is a robust guide on which whiskies to drink. His list of 'twelve names . . . which will probably win all but universal acceptance in representing Highland whisky at its most distinguished' is an impressive roll of honour which, the current fashion for Islay malts apart, would stand as a useful refresher to even the most experienced drinker.

In these pages, long-lost distilleries are brought to life and their merits discussed: there is much of value in the description of Islay and, even more poignant, Campbeltown whiskies. MacDonald's description of the Campbeltowns as 'the double basses of the whisky orchestra' is still quoted today and remains the classic descriptor of these 'potent, full-bodied, pungent whiskies'. How we now slaver for these lost glories. What the student of the cratur would not give to taste Rieclachan, Glenside or Benmore in their pomp!

He reminds us too, that whisky has changed. 'The convenient proximity of a peat bog is an economic necessity for a Highland malt distillery' is not a sentence that could, in truth, be written today and, in its very matter-of-factness, speaks volumes for the change in the taste of our drams. So too, the thought that Highland malts will affect a man leading a sedentary life by making him 'liverish'. This seems a curious observation from one who, as we shall see, lived entirely by the pen, but the peculiar idea that malt whisky is somehow too demanding for the effete office worker and demands the vigorous outdoor life of the Highlander of popular imagination has passed into mythology.[1]

Whilst this might seem an outlandish conception, vigorously refuted both by the growing legions of female malt drinkers and the enthusiasm with which ever-increasing levels of phenol are demanded in the newly fashionable malts of Islay, the thought must inevitably occur that perhaps our whisky *has* changed. Perhaps we are mere boys compared to MacDonald's heroic topers and, worrying thought, perhaps the price of whisky's world domination is that it *has* been rendered bland. These are deep matters to ponder, demanding the most pungent of drams to stimulate speculation, for truth lies deep in the bottle.

However, whilst we may look with nostalgia on Campbeltown's long-lost peat-soaked monsters, elsewhere we find mention of some 128 blends comprising a mixture of Scotch and Irish spirit. Theirs is a passing that cannot be lamented and, indeed, the ever-reliable MacDonald trenchantly casts them headlong with two words – they are, he tells us, the 'crowning horror' of blending.

Clearly no apologist for the blender, in this as so much else, he anticipates our zeitgeist. MacDonald is a single malt man and stout defender of the drinker against a conspiracy of silence that he describes as existing amongst blenders 'to prevent the consumer from knowing what he is drinking'. Well spoken, indeed.

His cry for clear labelling and precise descriptions is a modern one and the industry could do worse than consider his plea that each label on a bottle ought to contain 'the names of the malt whiskies . . . in the blend, and the exact percentage of grain spirit . . . it should state the number of years and months that the blend and each of its constituents has matured in cask'. Is this so unreasonable? As he notes, 'sound whiskies would only gain by it'.

A modest enough proposal yet, I have no difficulty in prophesying, one that will be ignored before it is stoutly resisted 'by a body of men so assured of their commercial acumen as those who comprise the whisky trade'!

The date of the original publication, 1930, is all the more significant, indeed extraordinary, when we consider the industry's distressed state at that time. The name 'Pattisons' still echoed ominously. This high-profile concern had driven ten other distillers into receivership, blackened the whole name of blending and, indirectly, led to a Royal Commission on Whisky following exposure at their criminal trial of the nefarious practices of their infamous blending vat.

The Pattison brothers may have been in jail by 1901, but their malign influence cast a long and dark shadow. Then, scarcely recovered from the Pattisons' blending scandal and subsequent crash, Scotch whisky faced the triple challenges of the Great War, the Great Depression and Prohibition in the USA, its most important market.

Between the beginning of the century and 1930 some fifty single malt distilleries were closed, many permanently (just one was opened). The industry in Campbeltown, once the most prosperous in the country, teetered on the brink of extinction. Whisky, today such an icon of national identity, was then in unparalleled crisis.

MacDonald's voice, then, stands alone and just when we might reasonably have expected whisky's valediction, his book was a passionate and keenly-felt rallying cry. However, it could be argued that books by earlier writers, such as Alfred Barnard, Professor George Saintsbury and

Captain W. Smith Grant, justify the accolade of being the first in this field. Hardly. Though hugely important, and rightly revered today, Alfred Barnard wrote for a trade audience in his *The Whisky Distilleries of the United Kingdom* (1887). It was a time of confidence and growth and his concern is with output, ownership and matters of business, whilst Grant's work, *Glenlivet: Where Romance and Business Meet* (1924), is a panegyric to one distillery only, coincidentally his own! A promotional booklet, however fascinating at this distance of time, is not to be compared with MacDonald's pioneering opus.

Saintsbury's *Notes on a Cellar-Book* (1923) must likewise be disqualified: merely eight pages are devoted to whisky. We devoutly wish for more but he is silent. There is, however, a tantalising link to this esteemed Grand Old Man of drink and letters: as the long-serving Professor of Rhetoric and English Literature at the University of Edinburgh he was well-known to the founders of the Porpoise Press, original publishers of *Whisky*.

They approached him, then aged eighty, in 1922 for an essay for the fledgling Porpoise, but were declined. *Notes on a Cellar-Book* was even then in preparation – is it fanciful to imagine him serving his young admirers a glass, or even exciting their youthful imaginations with daring talk of a whole volume on whisky?

Certainly, MacDonald stands in awe of the venerable

Professor, describing him as 'patriarchal', one who has 'not succumbed to the degeneracy of the age' and quoting with reverence Saintsbury's views on grain whisky ('only good for blending, or for mere "drinkers for drunkee"'). Later, Saintsbury is repeatedly invoked as an authority beyond reproach but, MacDonald's respect notwithstanding, Saintsbury's commentary on whisky is too slight to be compared to his follower's greater work.

Thus, *Whisky* stands alone in distinction even before we tackle the opening chapter. As the first modern book on whisky, and as the spiritual chief of all that follow, it commands our attention. But MacDonald's name does not reappear in literature after this single work. Who was this author, and why was he so curiously reticent?

Some detective work was required here and the answer is a fascinating one, for 'Aeneas MacDonald' proved to be the pseudonym of a very much more prolific and long-lived Scot, who adopted a *nomde plume* just once.

Enquiries to the Society of Authors were fruitless and an extensive search of web sources proved to be circular. To track MacDonald down and confirm his true identity required scouring the National Library of Scotland, the Faber & Faber archives and a database maintained by the University of Texas; finding an obscure and out of print academic monograph;[2] corresponding with the Garrick Club and others and persuading a variety of sources that they did indeed have helpful information, even if they did not recognise it as a piece in a larger jigsaw. Eventually, the search led to his daughter and – at last – it is possible to reveal the whole story.

Aeneas MacDonald was, in fact, George Malcolm Thomson, a Leither by birth, Dux of Daniel Stewart's College and, after brief service as a 2nd Lieutenant in the Great War, a graduate of Edinburgh University.Born in August 1899, Thomson had established the Porpoise Press in 1922 in partnership with his university friend Roderick Kerr and one John Gould, with an initial capital of twenty pounds.

However limited its assets, its aims were rather more ambitious: 'a serious though modest effort to create a publishing house in Scotland of distinction for original work.'

This bold manifesto was eagerly taken up by the Scottish press, the *Scots Pictorial* commenting favourably:

Everyday it is being borne more forcibly upon our minds that there is a great need for a Scottish literary and publishing centre such as the founders of the Porpoise Press are endeavouring to establish. For there are young literary men in Scotland whose work is known only to a small circle, because there is no proper medium by which it may be introduced to the larger public which may be eager to know it.

By 1930, the Porpoise Press had issued some forty-eight titles, mostly original poems and novels by Scottish authors including George Blake, Eric Linklater, Hugh MacDiarmid and Neil M. Gunn. Thomson himself had contributed two titles at this point: the broadsheet *An Epistle to Roderick Watson Kerr* (as Kerr had left Edinburgh to take up a position on the Liverpool *Daily Post*) and a Porpoise Pamphlet *Will the Scottish Church Survive?*

Thomson, by then an active journalist and author, had also written two other more significant works: *Caledonia, or the Future of the Scots* and *The Rediscovery of Scotland*, both in 1928 through the London publishers Kegan Paul, Trench, Trubner & Co., who issued his *A Short History of Scotland* in 1930.

The two earlier books attracted the attention of Lord Beaverbrook and, by 1930, Thomson had moved permanently to London to work for the *Evening Standard*. A long and distinguished career in journalism followed, interrupted only by work as one of Beaverbrook's closest advisors in various wartime ministries. This, and his lengthy retirement, was interspersed with some twenty books, mostly well-regarded political commentaries and historical biographies, and one novel, with a Jacobite theme, *The Ball at Glenkerran* (1982).

Having modestly declined a decoration for his war work, George Malcolm Thomson was appointed OBE in 1990 for services to journalism. He died in May 1996, aged ninety-six. Ironically for one described in his *Times* obituary as 'a Scot through and through', he remained in London until his death.

As a young man, he studied both History and English Literature at Edinburgh University. Perhaps it is here that we find the roots of his life-long fascination with Jacobitism and his strong sense of national identity. Certainly, the nationalist tone of the Porpoise Press fitted with the growing resurgence of native pride and a distinctive sense of a Scottish identity. It also chimed with the acceptance of youthful ideas prevalent in intellectual circles after the First World War, as the writers of the Kailyard were pushed aside in favour of a growingly self-conscious Scottish Renaissance.

Hugh MacDiarmid (C.M. Grieve) abandoned self-publishing in favour of the Porpoise Press and Neil Gunn moved from Jonathan Cape to the same publisher in acknowledgement of its overt 'consciousness of Scottishness', as George Blake expressed the spirit of the his age. George Malcolm Thomson's significance in all of this is forever immortalised by Lewis Grassic Gibbon's dedication to Thomson of his novella *Cloud Howe* (the second part of his trilogy, *A Scots Quair*).

But why adopt a pseudonym in the first place? The question is easily answered: Thomson's parents were strictly teetotal and anonymity was necessary to avoid offending his mother.

This is the explanation given by McCleery, historian of the Porpoise Press, who interviewed Thomson in August 1983. Thomson himself, in private correspondence with Neil Gunn in November 1930, wrote: 'Please keep my name out of 'Whisky' if you don't mind[3] . . . I have private reasons – and should hate people to think the P.P. existed to publish me alone.'

Shortly afterwards he wrote again to Gunn: 'My mother is coming down & as she is an ardent T.T. (Good God!) I am having my little dinner on Thursday 22nd in the Norwegian Club,[4] where the wine is good and abundant. You had better meet my wife, child & mother <u>for tea</u>!!'

Perhaps the formidable Mrs Thomson was appeased by a loyal son's dedication to her of *A Short History of Scotland* – none of his other earlier works carry any such inscription.

However, an additional factor may well have influenced Thomson: reaction to his earlier *Caledonia, or the*

Future of the Scots. Published in 1928, this attracted a certain controversy, with Thomson described as 'the best-hated man in Scotland'.

This book, and its immediate, more fully developed sequel *The Re-Discovery of Scotland*, show Thomson disillusioned with Scotland and all her works. *Caledonia*, indeed, is little more than a diatribe: passionate, forceful and well-argued though it undoubtedly is, one senses the disappointment of a young man whose ambitious plans for the Porpoise Press he believed dashed by the provincial philistinism of dour Edinburgh (a city 'dominated socially by a caste of sport-talking lawyers, doctors and insurance officials' – *The Re-Discovery of Scotland*).

Certainly his thoughts were already turning to London and, with such sentiments as '[Scotland] is a land of second-hand thoughts and second-rate minds' unlikely to win friends at home, there will have been many who heartily wished this brash young man on the first train to Kings Cross.

Is it fanciful therefore to surmise that in addition to avoiding the link between the family name and the demon alcohol, Thomson might have wished to prevent the opprobrium then attaching to *his* name from damaging the prospects for *Whisky* or, indeed, the Porpoise Press itself? For these were sensitive times in the life of the venture: by 1930, in recognition of the partners' burgeoning careers, largely out of Scotland, the house was being sold to Faber & Faber and he may have thought it prudent to avoid courting unnecessary controversy. Certainly this was a bitter pill for Thomson – much space in his earlier books is given over to castigating a lack of domestic industry and the dominance of England in Scottish life. To have to relinquish the Porpoise Press to a London house must have seemed a betrayal.

As late as April 1930, however, he still harboured ambitions for the Porpoise Press. Attempting to recruit Neil Gunn as an author he wrote: '. . . the books will make Scotland take us seriously but the pamphlets . . . will fill a gap in a Scotland which has no serious press'.[5]

Be that as it may, the name Aeneas MacDonald would have meant more – indeed would have been richly symbolic – to Thomson's contemporaries, especially those with strong nationalist leanings. A pseudonym is not casually chosen. In adopting a name with such resonance in Scottish history Thomson tells us something of himself: a Jacobite, a believer in lost causes, a patriot and also a survivor.

For the original Aeneas MacDonald played a small but pivotal role in one of the most romanticised, yet blood-soaked, episodes in Scottish history: a venture as ill-considered as it was daring. He was banker to the '45, one of Bonnie Prince Charlie's 'Seven Men of Moidart' – the

Parisian exiles who sailed from Nantes in July 1745 with Prince Charles Edward Stuart.

More potent yet for this association, the Jacobite party first landed on the island of Eriskay on August 2nd 1745 – Thomson's own birth date 154 years later, and a link of which he was no doubt keenly aware.

Distrusted and insulted by the ferocious Highland clan chieftains, MacDonald nonetheless followed 'Charlie' to the very end. Fortunately for him, he was in Barra expecting a consignment of Spanish gold as the Duke of Cumberland directed the butchery at Culloden. Later he was captured, stood trial for High Treason, found guilty, condemned to death but pardoned and released, to return to France.

In dressing in Jacobite clothing then, Thomson consciously takes on an identity entirely sympathetic to his own Scottish Renaissance and there are more than passing references to 'the '45' in *Whisky*:

Whisky found an honoured place in the commissariat of the Jacobite armies. It gave spirit and endurance to Montrose's men on those marvellous marches with which they confounded the hosts of the Covenant; it comforted the kilted soldiery on the mad memorable raid on Derby in 1745 and ministered to the Prince himself when he was a hunted man.

And, again, later in chapter two of this book: 'Now dawned the heroic age of whisky, when it was hunted upon the mountains with a price on its head as if it were a Stuart prince . . .'

But, before turning to *Whisky*'s continued cultural significance and contemporary importance, a note on its publishing history.

There have been three editions, though only two are generally known. The original, reproduced here in facsimile, is the first (and, until now, only) UK edition, published by the Porpoise Press of Edinburgh in Autumn 1930.

As described above, MacDonald/Thomson was one of the founders of the Porpoise Press, but by the time his book was published the business was in the process of being transferred to Faber & Faber. This first edition was published under the supervision of George Blake and Frank V. Morley of Faber. Printing was by Robert MacLehose & Co at the University Press, Glasgow, the first of many Porpoise Press titles to be produced there.

Whisky was published in an edition of 1600 copies – large, by Porpoise Press standards, with a blue linen cover, paper title slip on the spine and an attractive two-colour jacket faithfully reproduced in this Canongate edition. The illustration on the jacket, affectionately known as 'Cask Boy' (or 'Tipsy' to his friends), was drawn by A.E.

Taylor, who also contributed the distillery map. Interestingly, Tipsy today graces the packaging of Loch Fyne Whiskies' The Living Cask™, a special bottling named in homage to Professor Saintsbury's recommendation of vatted whiskies.

Tipsy also appears, but in monotone, on the dust-jacket of the first American printing of *Whisky*, published by Duffield & Green[6] of New York on 25th January 1934. The cover is brown linen, with gold lettering stamped on the spine for title, author and publisher together with a decorative thistle. Whilst the dust-jacket illustration is the same, however, the plates seem worn and some of the finer detail has been lost; A.E. Taylor's initials and the date, '30, have been removed from the illustration. The advertisements for other Scottish fiction on the rear of the jacket have also been dropped.

The US edition was also printed by MacLehose and appears internally identical to the UK version, with the exception of the distillery map. This has been simplified and re-drawn with many of Taylor's more artistic embellishments – such as the tiny sketches of bewhiskered kilted shepherds enjoying a dram – removed. Whilst much of the charm of the map is accordingly lost it must be conceded that it is rather easier to read!

Judging by the greater current availability of the American edition, its print-run was larger. With the ending of

Prohibition in December 1931, interest in drinks in the USA was very high and, despite the recessionary times, it seems that Duffield & Green risked a larger number of copies.

Until the present edition, then, these were the only printings of the full text of Aeneas MacDonald's *Whisky* – though in 1953 Thomson declined a proposal from The Grove Press of New York to issue a new edition, on the grounds that the text then required too extensive a revision. His identity was never revealed to them though.

However, there is a further and very rare edition of particular interest to both whisky enthusiasts and collectors of American literature – the 'Briefcase Breviary' (December 1930) by Henry & Longwell of Garden City, Long Island. Frank Henry and Daniel Longwell were employees of the publishers Doubleday, also based in Garden City. One of Doubleday's most renowned authors was Christopher Morley, the elder brother of Frank V. Morley, the director of Faber & Faber mentioned earlier.

A distinguished American journalist, novelist, playwright and poet, Morley was known for carrying a briefcase stuffed with books. Between 1928 and 1931 he, Henry and Longwell collaborated to create their own imprint, issuing slim limited editions they considered interesting, largely for friends. In mock salutation to

Morley's briefcase, these were known as 'Briefcase Breviaries', published by the 'firm' of Henry & Longwell.[7]

The edition, of just the first chapter, is bound in yellow boards, with a device resembling a shark's fin in black repeated across the cover. Produced on high-quality laid paper, just 307 copies were printed. Each is individually hand-numbered, with the following inscription:

307 copies privily printed,
300 for gainful traffic and 7 for hilarity,
December 1930, this being copy

Number......

THIS is an advance publication for a few connoisseurs
of the first chapter of Aeneas MacDonald's wise and
witty little treatise on Whisky which will later be
issued entire by other hands. The printers ave adhered
to the Scottish spelling of 'Whisky'; the United
States has now no right to insist on her
own traditional spelling 'Whiskey'.

Each copy is signed by the four protagonists immediately following the title page. Whereas Henry, Longwell and Morley's signatures appear confident and flowing, Aeneas

MacDonald's is more tentative and formal. On all the copies I have verified, the signature clearly reads 'McDonald' – a mistake unlikely to have been made by someone signing their own chosen alias and moreover a particularly improbable error for a passionate Scot. Did Thomson actually sign these or, as now seems more probable, did an American amanuensis perform this duty? If so, some minor literary subterfuge has just been uncovered.

I can only locate around twenty copies of the Henry & Longwell edition. Delightfully, number 1 remains in Christopher Morley's library at the Humanities Research Center of the University of Texas. This speaks eloquently of Morley's role in this little adventure and his enthusiasm for the book itself.

His place in the story of *Whisky* does not end there. In February 1934 in the *Saturday Review of Literature*, he 'puffed' the US launch:

Duffield & Green have published in full Aeneas MacDonald's admirable little panegyric on *Whisky*, one chapter of which was once privately issued under the furtive imprint of Henry and Longwell . . . 'Aeneas MacDonald' is an alias of a well-known Scottish writer whose other works are of an ecclesiastical nature.

The reference to MacDonald as an 'ecclesiastical' writer is an in-joke by Morley for those friends who shared the secret, and a droll reference to Thomson's Porpoise Pamphlet *Will the Scottish Church Survive?* It conveniently also served to throw others off the scent – successfully, as the true authorship of *Whisky* has never been widely known. Ingenious attributions include Neil Gunn[8] and Archie MacDonnell, Scottish humorist and author of *England, Their England*. At the very least, this putative author was a distinguished Scot of letters, and his initials seem to work!

Morley's was not the only review. The *New York Times* of 4th February 1934 contains a long and generous notice by Edward M. Kingsbury (a 1926 Pulitzer prizewinner). It is headlined *A* 'Great, Potent, Princely Drink' (a reference to MacDonald's opening paragraph) and strongly recommended 'Mr Aeneas MacDonald's Golden Treasury of Whisky Lore'.

Kingsbury quotes extensively from the text and, in rapturously praising the work, describes MacDonald as follows: 'The author of this little poem, essay, history, geography, treatise and manual is admirably named as well as fitted for this task of love. The Highlands speak to him. Like his Roman predecessor,[9] he brings back the old pieties and gods. There is something epic as well as georgic in his strain.'

He goes on to applaud MacDonald's 'subtle imagination',

commends many of MacDonald's remarks 'to our own distillers' (i.e. the US producers of bourbon and rye) and concludes: 'This is a small volume, but there are plenty of those who will love it. It is airy, witty, full of sound knowledge and practical wisdom.'

Edward Kingsbury, Christopher Morley and Neil Gunn were not the only contemporaries to appreciate the book. T.S. Eliot gave a copy to his close friend and mentor Harold Monro, of the Poetry Bookshop, inscribing it personally. So contemporary reaction was favourable, even if further editions did not appear.

But what is this to us? The world of whisky today is very different from 1930. Ownerships have changed along with distilling practice. Whisky has staged a recovery that would have delighted MacDonald. Publications on whisky abound. What can 'Mr Aeneas MacDonald's Golden Treasury' offer us today?

Lyricism, for one thing, principally in the prose. Too many of today's whisky books are little more than lists: handsomely produced, well-illustrated and comprehensive to a fault, but with the soul of a draper's catalogue. Others might be mistaken for material straight from the distillers' own amply-funded publicity machine and a third category distributes marks out of 100 to Glen This, Glen That and Glen Theother with the mechanical certainty of a drab provincial accountant.

Why any one 'expert' should be relied upon any more than the distiller's puff escapes me: in MacDonald's philosophy the enthusiastic drinker should learn and, thus informed, judge whisky for himself with 'his mother-wit, his nose and his palate to guide him'. Wise words.

All this is excellent stuff and confirmation, if any is needed, that MacDonald remains pertinent today. Indeed, with sound common sense he gives the recipe for a hot toddy; he anticipates the fashion for cocktails, whilst disparaging the then-fashionable mix of whisky and soda; his recommendations on blending your own whisky remain sound and his championing of the drinker against the complacency of an industry then in frightening decline is both robust and relevant.

Elsewhere in his work of this period, whisky is accorded relatively slight attention. In both *Caledonia* and *The Re-Discovery of Scotland*, Thomson is concerned with the decline in Scotland's major industries. In terms of sheer numbers of workers distilling has never competed with heavy industry, whereas in 1930 Scotland still had large-scale employment in shipbuilding, mining and fishing.

Now the two former industries are gone, undone by a toxic combination of under-investment, incompetent management and intransigent trade unions. Craven politicians, slavishly intent in making blood sacrifice to the great god Europe have all but finished off the latter.

So the 'Sixteen Men of Tain', heroes of a single malt's publicity, today assume a symbolic importance out of all proportion to their numbers. But distilling did not go entirely unnoticed in Thomson's two trenchant pleas for Scotland. In his *Caledonia* he observes that 'The whisky industry is in even worse plight, as a result of high taxation and American prohibition. In one important centre only one distillery out of seven is working.'

And in *The Re-Discovery of Scotland* his argument is backed up by cold statistics, chilling even today: 'In 1925, there were 124 distilleries working in Scotland; in 1926 there were 113. The export of whisky in 1926 was 800,000 proof gallons less than in 1925, and 1,856,000 less than in 1924.'

Enough. Today whisky is in robust health. 'Single whiskies', or malts as we now style them, take an ever-larger share of the market with a growing range of styles, ages and tastes. Close to 1,000 million bottles-worth of Scotch whisky is exported each year. New distilleries are being built and independent distillers once again opening their doors. Whisky is conquering new markets and making new friends. There are whisky magazines, newsletters and web sites; whisky festivals; whisky appreciation societies; even whisky auctions for whisky collectors (what do they drink? one wonders). 'Aeneas MacDonald' may rest easy.

George Malcolm Thomson may never have fully appreciated the significance of his little book, but he lives on through it and we are ever in his debt. We can no longer keep his name out of it, for he lit a torch that has burnt brightly ever since and still illuminates our faltering steps. His is truly a great, potent and princely voice that will not be stilled.

To think that he was frightened of his mother!

Ian Buxton, 2006

ACKNOWLEDGEMENTS AND NOTES

Particular thanks are due to Mrs Anne Ettlinger, George Malcolm Thomson's daughter, who authorised this new edition, shared reminiscences of her father, allowed access to his private correspondence and provided the picture of him. I am particularly grateful to Charles MacLean for his thoughtful Foreword, and his fellow whisky writers Dave Broom and Gavin Smith, who were generous with their encouragement: gentlemen, trebles all round! Steven Rothman, of Philadelphia, is currently preparing a new biography of Christopher Morley and freely shared his extensive knowledge and researches in the USA with me: I am in his debt. Faber & Faber freely allowed access to their archives. Finally at Canongate, Jamie Byng immediately and enthusiastically supported the project and Francis Bickmore was patient and conscientious – the very model of an editor.

1   It reappears as late as 1951 in Sir Robert Bruce Lockhart's *Scotch: The Whisky of Scotland in Fact and Story*

and S.H. Hastie's *From Burn to Bottle*. This latter was published by the Scotch Whisky Association, so presumably was then the authorised view of the industry. You may even catch, from time to time, a faint echo repeated today as a spurious endorsement of the 'manly' qualities of various single malts.

2   The history of the Porpoise Press is fully documented in *The Porpoise Press 1922-39* by Alistair McCleery (Merchiston Publishing, Edinburgh. 1988). This obscure academic monograph deserves to be better known as the only record of an important Scottish publishing house.

3   Gunn appears to have mentioned *Whisky* favourably in a review.

4   Thomson's wife, Else, was Norwegian.

5   Letter to Neil Gunn, 6th April 1930.

6   Little is known of this obscure American firm, which lapsed by 1936. Some papers survive in archives at Indiana University, but the publishing history of the US edition of *Whisky* appears to have been lost.

7   Their colophon echoed that of eighteenth-century publishers, with the inscription 'Publishers in Petto. Near the Cathedral, Garden City'. 'Petto' is a joke from the Latin meaning 'small' to suggest both the diminutive size of the editions and the scale of the business. Nonetheless, as recorded in Morley's daybook, they paid Thomson a royalty.

8   Gunn, of course, wrote his own *Whisky and Scotland* in 1935, Thomson writing to him 'My Dear Neil, Will you allow me to congratulate you on the whisky book. It is fine, really fine. I enjoyed it immensely.'

9   Understandably, the Jacobite allusion appears to have escaped the New York suburbanite.

WHISKY

WHISKY

By

AENEAS MACDONALD

EDINBURGH

CANONGATE BOOKS

CONTENTS

What sort of hivven's delight is this you've invented for all souls in glory ?

C. E. Montague

Sages their solemn een may steek,
An' raise a philosophic reek,
An' physically causes seek,
                    In clime an' season ;
But tell me whisky's name in Greek,
                    I'll tell the Reason.

Robert Burns

I

THE NATURE OF WHISKY

OF THE history, geography, literature, philosophy, morals, use and abuse, praise and scorn of whisky volumes might be written. They will not be written by me. Yet it is opportune that a voice be raised in defence of this great, potent, and princely drink where so many speak to slight and defame, and where so many glasses are emptied foolishly and irreverently in ignorance of the true qualities of the liquid and in contempt of its proper employment. For, if one might, for a trope's sake, alter the sex of this most male of beverages, one would say that there be many who take with them to the stews beauty and virtue which should command the grateful awe of men. Though, in truth, there is little of the marble idol of divinity about this swift and fiery spirit. It belongs to the alchemist's den and to the long nights shot with cold, flickering beams ; it is compact of Druid spells and Sabbaths (of the witches and the Calvinists) ; its graces are not shameless, Latin, and abundant, but have a sovereign austerity, whether the desert's or the north wind's ; there are flavours in it, insinuating and remote, from mountain torrents and the scanty soil on moorland rocks and slanting, rare sun-shafts.

But of those who contemn it a word. We shall describe them and, according to their deserts, either bid them begone or stay and be instructed. For the enemies of whisky fall under several headings.

There has of late come into being a class of persons who have learnt of wine out of books and not out of bottles. They are as a rule to be surprised drinking cheap champagne in secret but their talk is all of vintages and districts and *clos* and *chateaux*.

These dilettantes of the world of drinking are distinguished by weak stomachs and a plentiful store of snobbery. Wine merchants make of them an easy and legitimate prey. They are apt in quotation and historical anecdote, culling these from the books which honest men have written to advance the arts of civilization and to earn money. They roll great names on their tongues as though they were heralds marshalling the chivalry of France, or toadies numbering the peers they have fawned on.

In finding those qualities of bouquet and body which their textbooks bid them seek, they are infallible, provided the bottle has been correctly labelled. They will, indeed, discover them before they have tasted the wine.

One drinks ill at their tables ; it was in the house of such an one that an impolite guest remarked to his neighbour, ' This Barsac goes to my head like wine.'

These creatures have the insolence to despise whisky. Fresh from their conducted tour of the vineyards, the smellers of corks and gabblers of names sneer when its name is mentioned. It is, they declare, the drink of barbarians, offensive to the palate and nostrils of persons of taste ; above all, it is not modish. For all that is southern and Mediterranean is in the mode among us. Civilization is a Latin word and culture comes by the Blue Train. Better a rubber beach at Monte Carlo than all the sea-shores of the north. And, of course, we must affect enthusiasm for wine ; it is so European, so picturesque and cultivated. It shows one has a certain background. A cellar is like a pedigree and requires less authentication. Nor is actual experience of bibbing necessary ; a good memory and the correct books will suffice.

If one is actually forced to drink, one can toy for a time with the glass in one's palm, discuss the merits of the wine, quote from Brillat-Savarin and tell that anecdote about the Duc de Sully, open a learned debate on a possible incompatibility of temperament between the wine and the food with which it is proposed to wed it, and, when all else fails, confess to a delicacy of palate which the grosser forms of indulgence would outrage. By such stratagems are the absurd and unmanly inner weaknesses of the bookish wine snob concealed from the ridicule they deserve.

But let no man think that I would have the sublime impertinence to dispraise wine or attempt to compare things incomparable, and assuredly I do not criticize honest and discriminating lovers of wine who have learnt by original research and from the contents and not the labels of bottles. There is no quarrel between us. They are not to be found among the white-livered ranks of the traducers of whisky, whose excellences they will proclaim even when in the arms of their mistress.

I pass on to another type of enemy, the men who drink whisky. With pain and not without a hope that they may yet be saved, let us number their sins. Foremost among these is that they drink not for the pleasure of drinking nor for any merits of flavour or bouquet which the whisky may possess but simply in order to obtain a certain physical effect. They regard whisky not as a beverage but as a drug, not as an end but as a means to an end. It is, indeed a heresy of the darker sort, doubly to be condemned in that it lends a sad, superficial plausibility to the sneers of the precious. Whisky suffers its worst insults at the hands of the swillers, the drinkers-to-get-drunk who have not organs of taste and smell in them but only gauges of alcoholic content, the boozers, the ' let's-have-a-spot ' and ' make-it-a-quick-one ' gentry, and all the rest who dwell in a darkness where there are no whiskies but only whisky —and, of course, soda.

Yet it may be unjust to lay on the souls of such false friends the burden of whisky's present lamentable plight when it has become less a delight to the mouths of men than an item in a pharmacopoeia, and is drunk for all sorts of illegitimate reasons, as by journalists to quieten conscience, by the timid to avert catarrh, by inferior poets to whip up rhymes, and by commercial travellers to dull the memory of rebuffs.

For those whose business it is to encourage the sale of whisky are not without guilt in the matter. They bandy no words about the aesthetic aspect of their wares ; their talk is all of moral and physiological advantages : ' It does you good ' ; ' After a hot tiring day ' ; ' Now that the cold weather is coming ' ; ' The doctor recommends it.' This is to be deplored, for it plays directly into the hands of those who look on whisky at its lowest, as a mere brute stimulant, who believe that one bottle of whisky resembles another very much as one packet of Gold Flake cigarettes another packet of Gold Flake cigarettes, and whose nearest approach to discrimination is to say ' small Scotch (or Irish), please,' instead of the still more catholic ' a small whisky '.

As a result, there has been a tendency to abolish whisky from the table of the con- noisseur to the saloon bar and the golf club smoke-room. The notion that we can possibly develop a palate for whisky is guaranteed to produce a smile of derision in any company except that of a few Scottish lairds, farmers, gamekeepers, and bailies, relics of a vanished age of gold when the vintages of the north had their students and lovers.

14

It may indeed be that the decline of whisky as a civilized pleasure is linked with the decay of taste in Scotland. For it was from Scotland that first England and then the world at large acquired the beverage, though the Scots must share with the Irish the honour of being its first manufacturers. While a high standard of culture was still to be found in a Caledonia less stern and wild than to-day and whisky still held its place in the cellars of the gentry and of men of letters, who selected it with as much care and knowledge as they gave to the stocking of their cellars with claret, whisky retained its place as one of the higher delights of mankind. But when Scots opinion was no longer to be trusted, the standards of the whole world suffered an instant decline, similar to that which would befall Burgundy if the solid bourgeoisie of France and Belgium were to perish suddenly and no one was left to drink the wine but the English and the Americans.

And at last a day dawned when it became possible for the average Englishman to be ignorant of the very names of all but four or five blends of whisky (all of which stared at him in enormous letters from hundreds of hoardings) and for the average English public-house to stock no more than three or four proprietary brands. It is small wonder if, in the face of an indifference and promiscuity so widespread, the distilling firms relaxed their standards : no restaurant would trouble to lay in *Cabinett-wein* if its clients asked only for hock and would pay only one price whatever was brought to the table. Yet, at the same time, one cannot quite exculpate the whisky-makers from the guilt of having chosen the easier and more profitable path at the expense of the prestige of their own commodity. It was their duty to guard it jealously, for it cannot be maintained seriously that those who make the food and the drink of man are in the same category as mere commercial manufacturers. Theirs is a sacred, almost a priestly responsibility, which they cannot barter away for turnovers and dividends without betraying their trust as custodians of civilization. Flour and beef, wine, brandy, and whisky are not in the same category as Ford cars or safety pins. Or ought not to be.

It may be admitted, too, that there is some excuse for those who fall into the error of the whisky-swillers, who drink it because it has an infallible result, a loosening of the tongue, a dulling of the memory, a heightening of the temperature, or what not. For whisky—even inferior whisky—has a potency and a directness in the encounter which proclaims its sublime rank. It does not linger to toy with the senses, it does not seep through the body to the brain ; it communicates through no intermediary with the core of a man, with the roots of his consciousness ; it speaks from deep to deep. This quality of spiritual instancy derives from the physical nature of the liquid. Whisky is a re-incarnation ; it is made by a sublimation of coarse and heavy barley malt ; the spirit leaves that earthly body, disappears, and by a lovely metempsychosis returns to the world in the form of a liquid exquisitely pure and impersonal. And thence whisky acquires that lightness and power which is so dangerous to the unwary, so delightful to those who use it with reverence and propriety.

In the eyes of the uninstructed, whisky is a mere mitigator of the rigours of northern climates and northern theologies. This is an inaccurate or, at least, an incomplete view. The precise effects of whisky on the human organism, though they differ widely from those of wine, are not less complex. It is less adept in bathing with a rosy hue men and the works of this world ; it is not a protector of comfortable illusions. We do not find whisky drinkers discovering causes to love mankind which are not apparent to them when they cease to be under the influence of the spirit. They do not indulge in unreasonably optimistic visions of the beauty and perfection of things, nor do they sentimentalize over the supposed gaiety of a departed age. They do not bang mugs on the table and roar about the jolly Middle Ages ; they are not impressed by the well-padded spiritual comforts of Catholicism. Some might say that whisky is a Protestant drink, but it is rather a rationalistic, metaphysical and dialectical drink. It stimulates speculation and nourishes lucidity. One may sing on it but one is at least as likely to argue. Split hairs and schisms flourish in its depths ; hierarchies and authority go down before the sovereignty of a heightened and irresistible intuition. It is the mother's milk of destructive criticism and the begetter of great abstractions ; it is disposed to find a meaning—or at least a debate—in art and letters, rather than to enjoy or to appreciate ; it is the champion of the deductive method and the sworn foe of pragmatism ; it is Socratic, drives to logical conclusions, has a horror of established and useful falsehoods, is discourteous to irrelevances, possesses an acuteness of vision which marshals the complexities and the hesitations of life into two opposing hosts, divides the greys of the world rigidly into black and white. Foolishly regarded as the friend of democracy, it is as much the scorner of democratic fictions as of servility, snobbery, plutocratic stupidity and aristocratic arrogance. It is the banner of the free human spirit which refuses to be chained to the political expedients it is compelled to devise. ' Whisky and freedom gang thegither,' but the freedom is not a social myth or a national egotism but rather the profounder autonomy of the individual soul.

The English, who, by definition, will believe anything that the Scots tell them, took whisky from their northern neighbours. It is doubtful, all the same, if they have ever taken to it. The ale-sodden Saxon has a temperamental inability to comprehend the true inner nature of whisky, yet there is no doubt that it has given him, more or less against his will, a harshness and an edge alien to his original nature. It

has given him an Empire and the hobnailed
livers of his proconsuls. Sometimes he may
have wondered suspiciously what it really was,
this warlock liquor that came to him out of the
mists. How could the Scots, a disagreeable
people cringing under the tyranny of the pul-
pits, ever have come to think of this liberating
and audacious drink ? The Scots have perhaps
been misunderstood by the rest of mankind.
They are, for example, the most anti-clerical
people in the world. For what is the Presby-
terian system but a drastic putting of the
clergy in its place by the laity, a usurpation of
church government by the unordained ? They
have a deep but erratic strain of frivolity ; they
have never taken themselves seriously as a
nation ; their patriotism is of an impatient and
sporadic character. No one has ever doubted
their courage but none of the captains who led
them to battle could ever be sure whether they
would run away at first sight of the enemy or
remain and fight to the death. They were poor
material for military adventurers to work with
and they could never conceivably have had the
lack of humour which was required to build
the British Empire. The statute books of their
old parliaments are full of laws against golf

and football, for the Scots preferred these deplorably unwarlike sports to the practice of archery which would have fitted them for battle.

The gifts of Scotland to the world are strange indeed, if they come from a people serious to the point of gloom. What are they ? Whisky, golf, porridge, haggis, the kilt, the bagpipes, music hall comedians, public house jokes. A curious list of products for a staid and sober people !

But whisky now belongs not to the Scots but to the world at large. It has therefore to be examined in relation to mankind as a whole, that is to say to people who imperfectly understand its essential nature, who will regard it as a habit, mildly reprehensible or fortified by social sanctions, or as a medicine, who will not see in it an art or a science. The decline of whisky in our times may, therefore, be related to vagaries of the Zeitgeist more accurately than to commercial shortsightedness and the failure of an educated appreciation. This age fears fire and the grand manner, and whisky may have to wait for its apotheosis until there comes to life upon the globe a race of deeper daring which will find in the potent and fiery subtlety of the great spirit the beverage that meets its necessities.

But, in the meantime, what can be done by way of persuasion and exposition to rebuild the ruined altar of whisky, let us do.

II

HISTORY

THE ORIGIN of whisky is, as it ought to be, hidden in the clouds of mystery that veil the youth of the human race. Legend has been busy with it and has given it, like the Imperial family of Japan, an ancestor descended from heaven. Yet no Promethean larceny brought us this gentle fire ; whisky, or rather the whole art and science of distillation, was the gift of the gods, of one god, Osiris. The higher criticism may hesitate to probe a myth so poetic, may be content to hold its peace and accept the evidence of those X's on casks which have been adduced as direct links with the Osirian mysteries. It is certain, at any rate, that distilling is venerable enough to have acquired a sacred character. Whether it was born in the Nile Valley or elsewhere is a question of no consequence. The Chinese knew it before the Christian era ; arrack has been distilled from rice and sugar since 800 B.C. ; distilling was probably known in India before the building of the great Pyramid ; Captain Cook found stills in use among the Pacific islanders.

It has been held that those comparatively modern peoples whom we used to call the ancients knew nothing of distilling, but this view overlooks a passage in the *Meteorology* of Aristotle in which the father of scientific method notes that ' sea water can be rendered potable by distillation ; wine and other liquids can be submitted to the same process.' This seems at least to give brandy, and possibly whisky also, a place in the sun of Greek knowledge. But if lovers of whisky think to find a direct reference to their beverage in the fifth century Zosimus of Panopolis and his mention of the distillation of a panacea or divine water, they will make a mistake. Zosimus was not thinking of whisky. They may comfort themselves with the reflection that distillation from grain has normally preceded distillation from wine, as one might expect, the necessity of those who have no wine to drink being more insistent. The chances are, then, that whisky has a longer pedigree than brandy.

There is, in any case, a clearer reference to the brewing and distilling of grain liquors in the ancient world which opens the exciting prospect that Dionysos was the god of whisky before he was the god of wine. During his wars against the northern barbarians the emperor Julian the Apostate encountered and apparently tasted (and certainly disliked) a beverage made from barley. The occasion was celebrated in an epigram to this new or (as seems likelier) very old aspect of Dionysos which is found in the *Palatine Anthology* (ix, 368) and has been translated as follows in Miss Jane Harrison's *Prolegomena to the Study of Greek Religion* :

TO WINE MADE OF BARLEY

Who and whence art thou, Dionyse ? now, by
    the Bacchus true
Whom well I know, the son of Zeus, say : ' Who
    and what are you ? '
He smells of nectar like a god, *you* smell of goats
    and spelt,
For lack of grapes from ears of grain your
    countryman, the Celt,
Made you. Your name's Demetrios, but
    never Dionyse,
Bromos, Oat-born, not Bromios, Fire-born from
    out the skies.

It used to be thought that the early Thracian god, Dionysos Bromios, was connected with the loud peal of thunder, but as Julian points out, he was more probably associated with a grain-made intoxicant of the northern tribesmen. If the deduction is correct, it would explain the name Demetrios sometimes applied to the god, for Demetrios means ' son of Demeter ', the Corn-mother.

By what means the knowledge of distilling arrived at the twin nurseries of whisky from the East we know not. It is not absurd to conjecture that those Mediterranean trader-seamen who are known to the anthropologists under such a variety of names brought it with them when they came in search of tin and gold and the pearls of our rivers. It is—to shun the temptation of filling in the gaps of history—at least certain that distilling was known to the Celtic peoples at an early date. Taliesin, the Welsh bard of the sixth century, mentions the process in his Mead Song and hints at a widespread knowledge of it : ' Mead distilled I praise, its eulogy is everywhere.'

The scene shifts to Spain of the Moors and the twelfth century. Abucasis has been named the first philosopher of the West who applied distilling to spirits. In the following century Arnoldus de Villa Nova, chemist and physician, disciple of the learned Arabs, describes distilled spirit and calls it the ' water of life '. Raymond

Lully, chemist and philosopher of Majorca, praises the ' admirable essence ', describing it enthusiastically as ' an emanation of the divinity—an element newly revealed to man, but hid from antiquity, because the human race was then too young to need this beverage, destined to revive the energies of modern decrepitude'. The very accents of whisky advertising in our own days are caught here ; Lully was born six centuries too soon. But it turns out that Lully is not praising whisky. Let him describe the making of the elixir : ' Limpid and well-flavoured red or white wine is to be digested during twenty days in a close vessel by the heat of fermenting horse-dung, and to be then distilled in a sand-bath with a very gentle fire. The true water of life will come over in precious drops, which, being rectified by three or four successive distillations, will afford the wonderful quintessence of wine.'

Whatever the Arabs may have known, then, it is not proved that they anticipated the Scots and the Irish (or their Celtic ancestors) in the discovery of whisky. The whole problem is made more difficult by the fact that the early term for distilled spirit is sometimes used in Scottish and continental manuscripts for any kind of distilled spirit ; sometimes there is no doubt whatever that whisky is ' the water of life ' referred to and sometimes it is equally clear that brandy is indicated. There is a school which insists that *aqua vitae* is a corruption of *acquae vite*, ' water of the wine '. If this is indeed so, then it seems probable that in the earlier writers *aqua vitae* denotes a kind of brandy. But, on the other hand, the word ' whisky ' is derived from the Gaelic ' *uis gebeatha* ', which is ' the water of life ', a direct translation of the Latin *aqua vitae*.

Daring indeed is the man who will presume to take sides in a question of precedence between the Irish and the Scots. He is as likely to be damned for his interference by the one party as to be denounced for his partiality by the other. When therefore one records that whisky, authentic and indubitable, first enters history as a beverage in use among the Irish one hastens to add that this proves nothing against the Scots. The mere fact of the priority of written evidence may mean anything or nothing, and, in this case, the Scots have the powerful retort to throw at their rivals that the precedence is due only to the fact that the Irish were conquered earlier than the Scots and not

less effectively. Soon after the invasion of
Ireland in 1170 the English found the Irish
making and drinking what they called *aqua
vitae* but which is undoubtedly whisky. Probably it had been in use for centuries before
in Scotland as well as in Ireland, for it is hard
to believe that two peoples who had so much
to do with one another in the way of fighting,
trading, thieving, and combining to fight common enemies did not share with one another
their most prized possession.

At any rate in Skene's *Four Ancient Books of
Wales* it is stated that by the sixth century the
Gaels were known as skilled distillers. *The Red
Book of Ossory*, an Irish manuscript of the
fifteenth century, contains a detailed Latin
description of the method of distilling *aqua vitae*
and its employments as a medicine, but as this
spirit was made from wine at least a year old
distilled ten times, we deduce that the Hiber-
nian talent for distillation was not confined to
barley malt. Stanihurst, writing in the reign
of Queen Elizabeth, has a passage closely
parallel to that of the Irish scribe : ' One
Theoricus ', he says, ' wrote a proper treatise
of *aqua vitae*, wherein he praiseth it unto the
ninth degree. He distinguisheth three sorts,

simplex, composita, perfectissima. . . . Ulsta-
dius also ascribeth thereto a singular praise,
and would have it burn being kindled, which
he taketh to be a token to know the goodness
thereof. And trulie it is a sovereigne liquor if
it be orderlie taken.' In an early Latin *Life of
St. Brigida* we learn that the celebrated Celtic
saint, whose name is still remembered in
numberless wells in Scotland (and was there
not a Bridewell in London ?), re-performed the
miracle of Cana, the water being transformed
into a liquid more acceptable than wine to a
whisky-drinking people :

' *Christi autem ancilla videns quia tunc illico
non poterat invenire cerevisiam, aquam ad balneum
portatam benedixerit et in optimam cerevisiam con-
versa est a Deo et abundanter sitientibus propinata
est.*'

By the fifteenth century the manufacture and
use of whisky was well established in the Scottish Highlands and its fame had already penetrated to the Lowlands and the court of the
illustrious king James IV. The Scottish Ex-
chequer Roll of 1494-1495 informs us that eight
bolls of malt were delivered to one Friar John
Car to make *aqua vitae.* In 1497 a gift of whisky
was brought to the king at Dundee by a barber

who got 9s. for his courtesy. Exactly a century later Fynes Moryson, the traveller, reported that there was a distinction between Scotch and Irish whisky, the distinction being, he thought, in Ireland's favour. But in fairness to Scotland, it may be doubted if Moryson had tasted the best of the Scotch spirit. The Highlanders were notoriously reluctant to part with their finer whiskies. At this time there were three kinds of whisky known in the Isles, graded by their quality and by the elaborateness of the distilling process : usquebaugh, trestarig, and usquebaugh-baul. But these were mysteries still guarded by the Grampians and the Western Seas.

Not that whisky was completely unknown in England. In Henry VIII's reign Irish immigrants opened distilleries there and about the same time the South acquired a liking for the Scottish variety of the spirit. Shakespeare may have been referring to some inferior imported whisky in *As You Like It* :

> For in my youth I never did apply
> Hot and rebellious liquors in my blood.

If this be so, the dramatist was only repeating by insinuation counsel which was incorporated into actual law in the Hebrides in 1609. Nine years later, Taylor, the water poet, in describing a famous hunt in Mar, speaks of ' the most potent *aqua vitae* '.

Temperance legislation, which has pursued whisky and whisky's less intelligent admirers through the centuries, is first encountered in the fifth of the Statutes of Icolmkill agreed to by the Island chiefs. This statute pointed out that one cause of the poverty of the Isles was the immoderate consumption of *aqua vitae*. It restricted its manufacture for sale and imposed severe penalties on law breakers. But it permitted every man to distil as much as he liked for his own use. Several years later the Scots Parliament passed an ' Act that nane send wynes to the Ilis ', for the purpose of mitigating the deplorable events which are likely to occur when the grape is added to the malt of grain. There is evidence, too, for the belief that the Islesmen were not alone in discovering their whisky was intoxicating as well as delightful. The first specific mention of a man getting drunk on whisky occurred when Lord Darnley, the deplorable second husband of Mary Stuart, made one of his French friends drunk on *aqua composita*, a kind of whisky.

During the first half of the seventeenth century whisky's popularity grew in the Scottish Lowlands, especially in the west, which was in closer contact with the Highland distilleries. All along the Highland Line, where Saxon and Gael met, distilleries were springing up, making the spirit which was sold in Glasgow taverns. During the Restoration period, when deep drinking was as popular a form of reaction against an overdose of Puritanism in Scotland, as were wenching and play-going in England, whisky's fame spread. In the *Mercurius Caledonius* of 1661 there is an account of a race run by twelve browster wives, at the instigation of some young Edinburgh blades, from Portobello to the top of Arthur's Seat. The reward for the dame who finished first in this more than athletic test was a hundredweight of cheese and a budgell of Dunkeld *aqua vitae*. By this time whisky was being made in Morayshire, where there was a local variety known as ' burnt *aqua vitae* ', and in Glasgow, as well as in Dunkeld and other strictly Highland areas. But the distilleries were small and they catered chiefly for local needs. Probably the finest whiskies were distilled by Highland chiefs for the use of their own households ; the classic brands were still unknown.

As early as 1505 the Royal College of Surgeons at Edinburgh were given the monopoly of distilling and selling *aqua vitae* within the City bounds. If they had preserved this right, there would have been small need for the Edinburgh medical faculty to collect fees from their patients and perhaps the prestige of the Edinburgh medical school would never have been acquired. The first news we get of a really famous whisky is in 1690 when the ' ancient brewery of aquavity ' at Ferintosh, in the possession of the Whig Forbes of Culloden, was sacked by marauding Jacobite Highlanders and ' all the whiskie pits . . . destroyed '. In recompense Forbes, or Culloden as we should style him in the good Scottish territorial fashion, was given a ' tack ' or rent of the excise of the land. In effect, he was allowed to distil his whisky, already noted for its quality, without paying the excise on the malt. In a year or two it was said that as much whisky was distilled at Ferintosh as in all the rest of Scotland, and Culloden was making so much money that the Master of Tarbet complained to the Scots Parliament. But it was only in 1784 that the government compounded with Culloden for the exemption at a cost of £21,000. By that

time ' Ferintosh ' was almost as frequently used
to describe the spirit as ' whisky ' itself, and
Burns somewhat prematurely mourned the
passing of its ancient glories in his *Scotch Drink* :

> Thee Ferintosh ! O sadly lost !
> Scotland laments frae coast to coast !
> Now colic-grips an' barkin' hoast,
>   May kill us a' ;
> For loyal Forbes' chartered boast
>   Is ta'en awa !

An exciseman, writing in 1736 of the manners
of the Highlanders, pays a tribute to the virtues
of whisky : ' The ruddy complexion, nimble-
ness and strength of those people is not owing
to water-drinking but to the *aqua vitae*, a malt
spirit which is commonly used in that country,
which serves both for victual and drink.'
Whisky found an honoured place in the commissariat of the Jacobite armies. It gave spirit
and endurance to Montrose's men on those
marvellous marches with which they confounded the hosts of the Covenant ; it comforted the kilted soldiery on the mad memorable
raid on Derby in 1745 and ministered to the
Prince himself when he was a hunted man.
He had already tasted it in Culloden House on
the eve of the fatal battle. It is reported that on

one occasion he and two others finished the
bottle at a sitting, the Prince consuming more
than half the contents. When the ' Highland
Host ' came to Ayrshire to plague the stubborn
West-country Whigs, William Cleland said
that each man of theirs thought his flask of
whisky as essential a part of his military equipment as his claymore :

> There's yet I have forgotten
> Which ye prefer to roast or sodden,
> Wine and wastle, I dare say,
> And that is routh of usequebay.

The verses are poor things ; the observation
was no doubt accurate.

Smollett says that ' The Highlanders regale
themselves with whisky, a malt spirit as strong
as Geneva, which they swallow in great quantities without any signs of inebriation.' That
they had many opportunities for doing so, we
gather from *The Lyon in Mourning* which snob-
bishly dismisses the hospitality of Skye, ' all the
publick houses there being mere whiskie
houses '. But it is doubtful if the Highlanders
were so free from the consequences of over-
indulgence in whisky as Smollett would have
us believe. There is evidence that the crafty
Hanoverians found a way of employing whisky

to loosen Highland tongues and loyalties, as a letter written by Lieutenant-Colonel Watson from Fort Augustus in 1747 shows : ' How soon the posts are fixed the commanding officer at each station is to endeavour to ingratiate himself in the favour of some person in his neighbourhood by giving him a reward, or by filling him drunk with whisky as often as he may judge proper, which I'm confident is the only way to penetrate the secrets of these people.'

But whisky has a graver and more honourable association with the Jacobite romance than any that has yet been mentioned. On the crucial night before Culloden, when Prince Charles was drinking in Culloden House, other men were finding a strange and sacred use for whisky. In Bishop Forbes' *Journal* we read : ' Mr. John Maitland, chyrurgeon for the Soule . . . a Presbyter of the Episcopal Church of Scotland . . . was attached to Lord Ogilvie's regiment in the service of Prince Charles, 1745. He administered the Holy Eucharist to Lord Strathallan on the Culloden field (where that gallant nobleman received his death wound), it is said, with oat cake and whisky, the requisite elements not being attainable.'

During the greater part of the eighteenth century whisky was, in the Lowlands, an entirely unfashionable drink. Yet here one must distinguish. The cheap, popular whisky, distilled by Robert Stein at Kilbagie, who was easily the largest manufacturer, was poor stuff, worth no more than the penny a gill it fetched. It was this raw, fiery tipple that the claret-drinking Lowland gentry and professional people despised and this, no doubt, that the mob in Aberdeen tossed off in half mutchkins to celebrate the acquittal of Lord George Gordon in 1781. But the cultivated taste of the lairds and the merchants did not reject the finer whiskies —when they could be obtained. ' Whisky in these days,' says a writer on Glasgow clubs of the eighteenth century, ' being chiefly drawn from the large flat-bottomed stills of Kilbaggie, Kermetpans, and Lochryan, was only fitted for the most vulgar and fire-loving palates ; but when a little of the real stuff from Glenlivet or Arran could be got it was dispensed with as sparing a hand as curaçoa or benedictine.'

These were the days of great drinking in the North, when Smollett's Highland gentleman in *Humphrey Clinker* spoke for his class in thinking it a grave disparagement of his family that not

above a hundred gallons of whisky were consumed at his grandmother's funeral, and when
an ancient retainer pleaded with the guests at
his master's funeral, ' that it might never be
said to the disgrace of the master's hospitality
that any gentleman that was his guest got to
bed otherwise than being carried '. Whisky
and funerals appear to have had a particularly
close connection, for we have another account
of a similar servant who barred the exit to the
guests with the solemn words : ' It was the
express will o' the dead that I should fill ye a'
fou' and I maun fulfil the will o' the dead'. Need
it be said that the pious duty was performed to
the letter ? ' I assure you, Sir,' said Bozzy to
his mighty patron and victim, ' there is a great
deal of drunkenness in Scotland.' Whereupon
the Doctor uttered this majestic and memorable tribute to Scottish doggedness and capacity : ' No, sir, there are people who died of
dropsies which they contracted in trying to
get drunk.' But that may merely be an expression of Johnson's contempt as a port-loving
Englishman for what was in these days the
main beverage of the upper-class Scotsman.
(' Claret for boys '.) Whisky must not be
blamed for the intemperance of eighteenth

century Scotland, when judges took their bottle
of claret with them into court and when the
enlightened opinion on the use of alcohol might
be found in the profound remark of a Lord of
the Court of Session (himself no whisky-drinker)
in addressing a jury : ' It is said, gentlemen,
that the accused perpetrated this atrocious deed
when he was drunk. Gentlemen, if he would
do this when he was drunk, what would he no'
do when he was sober ! '

Powerfully assisted by the taxes on malt and
ale, the popularity of whisky spread in Lowland
Scotland during the second half of the eighteenth century. Yet the whisky which thus
conquered new territories was the rawest,
cheapest, and nastiest of its kind, consumed
because it produced the desired result of
drunkenness more speedily and economically
than ale. Unfortunately, too, when whisky
found its way into literature after so many
centuries of exile, it was praised by poets whose
taste was unlikely to be discriminating. Robert
Fergusson, the impoverished Edinburgh clerk,
certainly did not drink himself into Bedlam on
Glenlivet ; Burns, the arch-propagandist of the
spirit, was an Ayrshire peasant with a peasant's
taste for what was fiery and instant. It is

probable that the poet laureate of whisky had
but the slightest acquaintance with a whisky
pleasing to civilized palates and that his muse,
as he calls it, was nothing but the abominable
Kilbagie of his day. No word of Burns' gives
the slightest impression that he had any interest
in the mere bouquet or taste of what he drank ;
on the contrary, his eloquent praise is lavished
on the heating, befuddling effects of whisky.
If this was all that Burns sought, it would be
idle to suppose that he had any real appreciation of the merits whisky might have. And
Burns' attitude to whisky has, through the extraordinary popularity of his verse, become almost
universal. Whisky has been sung into fame
as a ploughman's dram.

The taxes on native liquors and the duties
on foreign spirits gave whisky such a swift popularity in the eighteenth century that it became
in its turn an object of taxation. The earliest
known excise of twopence per gallon was imposed in 1660 ; when English enthusiasm for
the drink awakened, an import duty of half a
crown a gallon on Scotch whisky was introduced. Immediately a great smuggling trade
sprang up—as much as 300,000 gallons crossed
the Border in one year. Then came the

charging of a license duty on the contents of
the still used by the distillers—ingeniously cir-
cumvented by the Scots, who altered their stills
so as vastly to increase the speed of production.
The net result of all this legislation was to
create an immense illicit distilling industry in
the Highlands. As late as 1820 at least half the
whisky sold came from unlicensed distilleries.
In 1814 all distillation in the Highlands in stills
of less than 500 gallons was prohibited. But
it was almost as impossible to make such legislation effective as it is to prevent a free American citizen from killing himself with the hip-
flask horrors of the era of Prohibition. There
were thousands of stills in the glens and the
shielings, and not all of the whisky they made
was bad. Much of it, on the contrary, was
better than the products of the licensed distilleries, for it was made in parts of the country
where the science of distilling, like the art of
playing on the bag-pipes, was an immemorial
tradition, and where the qualities of water and
soil favoured it.

Now dawned the heroic age of whisky, when
it was hunted upon the mountains with a price
on its head as if it were a Stuart prince, when
loyal and courageous men sheltered it in their

humble cabins, when its lore was kept alive in secret like the tenets of a proscribed and persecuted religion. If whisky has not degenerated wholly into a vile thing in which no person of taste and discernment can possibly take an interest, it is because its tradition was preserved, by men whose names ungrateful posterity has forgotten, during years when the brutal and jealous Hanoverian government sought to suppress in the Highlands this last relic of the ancient Gaelic civilization. It is an extraordinary thing that, while Jacobite loyalty has found its bards, this loyalty to a thing far more closely linked with Highland history than a Lowland family ever could become, has not yet been sung.

In 1814, we have noted, all distillation from stills of less that 500 gallons capacity was prohibited within the Highland Line ; the result of this piece of inequitable legislation was that in 1823 there were 14,000 charges of illicit distilling as compared with a total of six charges fifty years later. Still licenses were abolished in 1817 so far as Great Britain was concerned, but they remained in Ireland. The development of whisky distilling during the nineteenth century took very different paths in Scotland

and in Ireland. In the former country the small, illicit home still was supplanted by large, commercial distilleries ; in the latter, licensed distilleries grew fewer but the amount of illicit ' poteen ' distilling probably remained constant. In 1799 there were 87 distilleries in Scotland ; in 1817 there were 108 ; in 1825, there were 329 ; in 1833, there were 243 ; and in 1908, there were 150. In 1779 there were no fewer than 1,152 licensed stills in Ireland ; by 1800 this had fallen to 124 ; and by 1908 to 27.

So far as Scottish whisky is concerned, the era of the illicit distillers, the so-called ' smugglers ', is of capital importance. For it was they and not the large-scale purveyors of cheap whisky who kept alive an educated taste in whisky and the true traditions of its manufacture. It is significant that the chief centres of the ' smuggling ' have become classic districts of whisky, Glenlivet, Strathden, the Glen of New Mill. Glenlivet became the centre of the smuggling industry of the North. The farmers of the glen, discovering that a demand for their product was springing up in the outside world, made up parties with trains of pack-animals laden with the products of their stills to carry the whisky over the mountains to the

44

South. ' We have seen ', says a contemporary, ' congregations of daring spirits, in bands of from ten to twenty men, with as many horses, with two ankers of whisky on the back of each horse, wending their way, singing in joyous chorus, along the banks of the Aven.'

To those pious law-breakers, who were more exercised in spirit because the necessities of their mystery compelled them to work on the Sabbath than because it brought them under the notice of the excise department, the modern connoisseur of whisky owes a deep debt. As late as the 'twenties of last century there was no legal distillery in Glenlivet, where 200 illicit stills were at work. The Duke of Gordon, who was the principal landowner in the glen, told the House of Lords bluntly that the Highlanders were born distillers ; whisky was their beverage from time immemorial ; they would have it and would sell it too, when tempted by high duties. But if the legislature would pass an act making it possible to manu- facture whisky as good as the 'smuggled' product on payment of a reasonable duty, he and his brother-proprietors of the Highlands would use their best endeavours to put down smuggl- ing and to encourage legal distilling.

The government took the hint and the result was an act of 1823 sanctioning legal distilling at a duty of 2s. 3d. per gallon of proof spirit, with a license of £10 for each still over forty gallons. Smaller stills were made illegal. This act is of capital importance in the history of whisky. It imposed moderate instead of grotesque burdens on the industry. And, at the same time, it killed whisky-distilling in the home as distinct from the factory. But it could not have succeeded in this, had it not tempted enterprising individuals to undertake the manufacture of high-quality whisky. This, it was clear, could only be done in the areas where, as the ' smugglers ' had proved, natural conditions favoured production. The first man to open a licensed distillery upon this sacred soil was Mr. George Smith, whose courage, both physical and commercial, should be remembered gratefully by all who have tasted that great whisky, ' Smith's Glenlivet '.

George Smith was born in 1792, the son of a Glenlivet farmer. He was an educated man of good family and the possessor of an excellent Latin style ; he was in the beginning an architect and builder. But on his father's death he took over the farming of Upper Drumin, which, like his neighbours, he combined with illicit distilling of whisky. In the year after Waterloo the output of his ' bothy' was a hogshead a week. Mr. Smith has himself told the rest of his story :

' At length, in 1824, I, George Smith, who was then a powerful robust young fellow, and not given to be easily " fleggit," determined to chance it. I was already a tenant of the Duke, and received every encouragement in my undertaking from his Grace himself, and his factor, Mr. Skinner. The lookout was an ugly one, though. I was warned before I began by my civil neighbours that they meant to burn the new distillery to the ground, and me in the heart of it. The laird of Aberlour presented me with a pair of hair-trigger pistols, worth ten guineas, and they were never out of my belt for years. I got together three or four fellows for servants, armed them with pistols, and let it be known everywhere that I would fight for my place till the last shot. I had a pretty good character as a man of my word, and through watching, by turn, every night for years, we contrived to save the distillery from the fate so freely predicted for it.

' But I often, both at kirk and at market, had

rough times among the glen people ; and if it had not been for the laird of Aberlour's pistols, I do not think I should have been telling you this story now. In 1825 and '26 three more small legal distilleries were commenced in the Glen ; but the smugglers succeeded very soon in frightening away their occupants, none of whom ventured to hang on a single year in the face of the threats uttered so freely against them. In 1825 a distillery which had just been started at the head of Aberdeenshire, near the Banks o' Dee, was burned to the ground with all its out-buildings and appliances, and the distiller had a very narrow escape from being roasted in his own kiln. The country was in a desperately lawless state at this time. The riding officers of the revenue were the mere sport of the smugglers, and nothing was more common than for them to be shown a still at work, and then coolly defied to make a seizure.'

The task of the revenue officers in the Highlands, as they complained in 1784, was made more difficult because the distilleries were strategically situated on high ground which could not be overlooked. The surrounding lands were usually owned by the proprietors of the distillery who declined to allow the

officers to build their houses in the vicinity.
And, finally, large and fierce dogs were
loosed upon any unwelcome visitors to the
distillery.

The illicit distilling of Scotch whisky was
not confined to the Highlands. There were
400 unlicensed stills in Edinburgh in 1777,
when the number of licensed stills was only
eight. In 1815 a ' private ' distillery of considerable size was found under an arch of the
South Bridge in the Scottish capital. The
only entrance was by a doorway situated at
the back of a fireplace in the bedroom of a
house adjoining the arch. Water was obtained
from one of the mains of the Edinburgh Water
Company which passed overhead, and the smoke
and waste were got rid of by making an opening in the chimney of an adjoining house and
connecting to it a pipe from the distillery. In
the mid-nineteenth century a yet more scanda-
lous instance of the Scottish aversion from
paying duties occurred in Edinburgh when a
secret distillery was found in the cellars under
the Free Tron Church. But by that time the
battle for legalised distilling had been won.
It would no longer be the case that the finest
whiskies could only be obtained by dubious

and subterranean means from sources which could be but vaguely conjectured.

The modern history of whisky is so intimately associated with the development of manufacturing processes, with the commercial and financial aspects of what has become almost as much a science as an art and an industry rather than either, that it may be considered more conveniently under separate headings. We leave the story of whisky at a moment when it is exchanging a past illustrious and obscure for a present infinitely more prosaic, conducted in the full glare of modern commercialism and with all the devices at the disposal of a highly-capitalized, well-organized, large-scale industry. Whisky emerges from the shadows of the hermetic arts into the harsh limelight of the age of trusts and cartels and mass-production. The blue smoke rising warily above the heather dissolves and in its place there rises the gigantic image of one whose monocle, scarlet coat, top boots and curly-brimmed tall hat seem strangely remote from the glens and the clachans.

III

MAKING AND BLENDING

SOMETHING of a noble and elegant simplicity characterizes the apparatus employed in the manufacture of whisky. Reduced to its bare essentials it consists of two main instruments, the *still* and the *worm condenser*. The still is a retort of copper with a broad, rounded bottom and a tapering neck. The worm condenser, connected to the still by a short pipe, is a spiral tube, also made of copper. There is nothing vital in the equipment of a distillery which a village blacksmith could not make and a small cottager could not buy. Moreover, no marked improvement of any note has been made in the machinery of whisky-distillation during long centuries. We can now make purer industrial alcohol, we have perfected the technique of treating the barley and making the malt, we understand something more of the chemical processes which take place when whisky is produced, we leave less to chance than our fathers did, but we have not devised a still which will make better whisky than the old pot still which has been in use since the dawn of our knowledge of whisky, and we have not been able to construct a more practical method of condensing the vapour of the still than the worm pipe kept cool by running water. The Highlander of the fifteenth or sixteenth century might be bewildered for a few moments if he were suddenly introduced into a modern malt distillery but he would speedily recognise in their larger bulk and greater elaboration the familiar instruments from which he was accustomed to obtain his beloved usquebaugh.

There are two main descriptions of whisky, depending on the raw materials used. Whisky is either made from barley malt alone (the great Scottish whiskies all belong to this class) or from a mixture of barley malt with unmalted grains of different sorts (all—or almost all—Irish whiskies come under this category). The process of distillation may best be studied by observing the manufacture of a pure malt whisky, such a whisky as will be found by the fortunate possessor of one or other of the classic brands. The essentials of the manufacture are as follows :

The barley is brought from the farm into the barley-receiving room of the distillery where t is cleansed by being passed through screens ; the smaller, inferior grains are discarded. The selected barley is then taken in bags into a barn from which it passes into the malt house.

Here it falls into tanks called ' steeps ' where it is soaked in water. The softened, swollen grain is spread out on a malting floor for about three weeks, being sprinkled with water at regular intervals and occasionally turned over. As a result of this, the barley begins to grow or germinate.

When the proper time has arrived the water supply is shut off ; growth stops immediately and the grown barley is withered. In this state it is known as ' green malt '. What has actually been happening is that the starch of the barley has been partly converted into sugar by means of the ferment whose technical name is *diastase*.

The next step in the process is that of drying in the kiln. This is a supremely important operation for it is at this time that the malt acquires characteristics of flavour which it will later on impart to the whisky. Thus the chief distinction between the two main classes of Scotch whisky, Highland and Lowland, is that the former has its malt dried by means of peat

fires. The combustion gases of the peat endow
the whisky with that subtle ' smokiness ' which
is present, in discreet combination with other
flavours, in genuine Highland whisky.

The kilned malt passes into the mill room
where a wire screen removes the ' culm ' or
sproutings produced during malting. The
malt is ground in a mill. It is now passed into
the mashing tuns where it is thoroughly mixed
with warm water. Being later cooled, the
resulting liquid, known as *wort*, is drawn off.
The mashing process enables the diastase to
convert the remainder of the starch in the malt
to sugar and to *dextrine*, which dissolves in the
wort. The wort passes through a refrigerator
in the tun (or fermentation) room on its way
to the wash backs, yeast being added to the
liquor on the way. Fermentation now takes
place, the sugary substance in the wort being
transformed by the yeast into alcohol and
carbonic acid gas. The diastase converts the
dextrine into sugar, which the yeast in its turn
converts into alcohol.

The wash, or alcohol-containing liquor from
the fermentation room, is now introduced into
the wash still. This is the crucial operation,
for now the liquid, leaving the world of earthly

things behind, enters the realm of spirit. The result of the first distillation is a weakly alcoholic distillate known as *low wines*, which, after being condensed in the worm, passes to a receiver in the spirit-receiving room and is then returned to the spirit still in the still house to be re-distilled. This time the distillate is collected in two parts.

In the spirit-receiving room is a glass case known as the spirit safe where the specific gravity of the distillate is tested. The first portion of the second distillate is whisky and is passed into the spirit receiver ; the second, known as *feints*, contains alcohol in considerable proportion and passes into the low wines receiver where it is mixed with the next charge of low wines for re-distillation.

The finished whisky flows into a spirit vat in the spirit store and is poured into wine-saturated casks where it will mature. The function of these casks—they are generally sherry casks—is often misunderstood. They do not impart qualities to the whisky which it did not possess before, although the action of a saturated cask may be to conceal, under a strong, imported, winey flavour, some defects in an inferior whisky. But the casks give

colour to whisky, which in its native state is a
wholly colourless liquid. Why this austere
achromatism of whisky should be unpopular is
not easily to be explained. It may be that the
unearthly pallor of the pure and fiery spirit
strikes terror into the heart of man, as the
whiteness of the whale alarmed Captain Ahab
and his ship's company. (But why, then, does
no one protest against the colourlessness of
gin ?) It may be that whisky was originally a
' doctored ' spirit, containing in addition to
malt distillate, spices and other extraneous
flavouring and colouring matter. It may be
that the idea of drinking whisky made solely
from malt or grain is quite modern. There is,
indeed, some evidence for a popular, as distinct
from a learned, taste for spiced usquebaugh.

In George Smith's *A Compleat Body of Distilling*, published early in the eighteenth century, there is a recipe for ' Fine Usquebaugh '.
It contains six gallons of proof molasses-spirit,
six gallons of proof rectify'd spirit, and a whole
gorgeous East of condiments,—mace, cloves,
nuts, cinnamon, ginger, coriander seed, cubebs,
raisins, dates, liquorice, best English saffron,
and Lisbon sugar. Clearly the ingenious Mr.
Smith was only providing a home-made sub-

stitute for usquebaugh, but he could hardly have included spices unless he were seeking to imitate flavours which could hardly exist in an unadulterated whisky. His inclusion of saffron is also significant, for this would give a colour resembling that of modern whisky. In the North and the West, where spices were hard to come by, pure whisky, deriving its flavour from moss-water, peat and barley malt and from nothing else, first came into being and its high qualities were first recognized. But the prejudices of the Lowland and English market had to be considered, and so (we may conjecture) dyed whisky was manufactured. To this day Highlanders do not exhibit the aversion from colourless whisky that is so common among Lowlanders and Englishmen. (And, it may be observed in passing, fluid caramel or paxarette is frequently added to give whisky the complexion which it is supposed to derive from residence in sherry-casks.)

It is not to be thought, however, that the wine-casks do nothing more to the whisky than give it a tint. The wine-soaked wood of the casks absorbs various insoluble bodies which would otherwise mar the flavour of the matured whisky.

The manufacture of Irish whisky closely resembles that of Scotch except that, instead of barley malt, a mixture of malted and unmalted barley, wheat, oats, or rye, is mashed together. The diastase in the malt is sufficient to cause the breaking down of the starch in the unmalted grain into sugars, the subsequent conversion into alcohol being performed by yeast, as before. The process of distilling is carried out in pot-stills, whereas the Scotch grain whiskies are made in patent stills.

The first patent still to come into wide use was that invented about 1826 by Robert Stein of the celebrated Scottish family of whisky distillers. At that time there were 114 distilleries in Scotland, of which five were making for the English market. All of these were owned by the Stein family or by three firms of the name of Haig. Stein speeded up the working of the still by bringing steam into contact with the wort. The idea was developed later in the famous patent still of Mr. Aeneas Coffey of the Dock Distillery, Dublin. This was invented in 1830 and replaced Stein's patent. Coffey's still consists of two columns, the *analyser* and the *rectifier*. In the first of these, previously heated wort is passed downwards over a series of perforated copper plates, and meets an upward current of steam which carries off the alcohol from the wort. This is condensed at the bottom of the rectifier (the second column) on another series of perforated plates, this time cool plates, where it is collected in two portions, an upper consisting of more volatile alcohol and a lower known as *hot feints*. By this type of still it is possible to produce in one continuous operation a spirit containing 95 per cent. of alcohol. Coffey's still is therefore the means by which the greater part of our industrial alcohol is manufactured. Its value in whisky distilling is more doubtful. For whisky derives its character—or, rather, whiskies derive their characters—from the presence in the finished liquid of tiny ' impurities ' which the hard efficiency of the patent still eliminates.

The problem of whether or not spirits made in a patent still were entitled to the name of whisky is one which at one time exercised the minds of those who were genuinely interested in the honour of the liquid. It is difficult not to regret that the battle went on that occasion to the strong in numbers and wealth, and that the final decision was in the hands of those who were ignorant of what whisky really is.

It is unfortunately true that the whole modern history of whisky is a record of the opening of door after door to commercial vandalism, of the stretching of definitions until they cease almost to have any meaning at all. The influence of the patent still is not the only one to be deplored. Whisky has shown, or has been compelled to show, such a hospitality to strangers that its house has now an excessively crowded and variegated appearance. As early as 1678 the principal materials used in making Scotch whisky had been fixed, though herbs and spices were probably added as in Ireland to produce the various local brands of aqua vitae, cordial, etc. Sir Robert Moray writes, ' Malt is there (in Scotland) made of no other grain but barley whereof there are two kinds, one which hath four rows of grain in the ear, the other, two rows. The first is more commonly used ; but the other makes the best malt.' In the first half of the eighteenth century the ' Society of Improvers in Agriculture ' took up the question of whisky distilling ; one James Dunbar made suggestions about the manu-facturing process and a Dutchman, Wyn-

gaarden, drew up directions for the use of
Scottish distillers. Unscrupulous manufacturing methods were not a crime of the Highlanders, who protested that the spirit made in
the Lowlands, and in Ireland, from unmalted
grain was ' Scotch'd spirit ', not whisky.
Until quite late in the century Irish usquebaugh
was a cordial made by adding cinnamon,
liquorice, and other spices to grain or malt
spirit. It seems possible that in Scotland aqua
vitae referred to a pure malt spirit, and
usquebaugh to a spiced cordial ; at any rate
a distinction of some sort was preserved, for
in 1732 the Duke of Atholl wrote to Lord
George Murray, the famous general of the '45,
complaining that ' I have not one drop of
either usquba or acquvitae in the house.' In
the early part of the nineteenth century the
words ' Scotch whisky ' had a very definite and
precise meaning. They denoted a whisky
made in Scotland from malted home-grown
barley (dried over a peat fire in the case of
Highland whisky), and distilled in a pot-still.
At the same time Irish whisky had a similarly
close and exact definition. It meant whisky
made in Ireland by treble-distilling, in pot-
stills heated by furnaces, of a wort obtained

from a mash of malted barley, barley and oats, all the grain being home-grown.

As the century progressed, however, it became obvious that these definitions could not be adhered to. By the '70's it could no longer be concealed that much of the barley used in making Scotch whisky was grown abroad. This was a grave breach with tradition, for as early as 1703 the bailies of Strath Spey decreed that aqua vitae was to be brewed only from malt grown in the locality.

The introduction of patent still distilling had an even more disturbing effect in the art of whisky-making. For if a patent-still spirit was a whisky, then where was the line to be drawn ? Only by wresting the name ' whisky ' violently from its earlier, well-established meaning could it be applied to the neutral, ' silent ', flavourless product of the patent still. Adam Young in his *Distillery Instructions* refuses the name whisky to patent still spirits ; as late as 1890 it was widely and authoritatively denied.

But the Royal Commission on Whisky of 1908-1909 opened the dykes to the invading floods of patent-still spirit by defining whisky as ' a spirit obtained by distillation from a mash of cereal grain, saccarified by the diastase of malt. ' This was comprehensive enough, and sweeping enough. It made no distinction between Scotch and Irish whiskies ; it did not stipulate that the grain or malt should be home grown ; it did not specify that pot-stills alone were to be used ; it did not mention Scotch whisky's true character as a distillate of a wort made from malt. As one commentator has sardonically observed, it was at least something that beetroot, potatoes, and sawdust were eliminated. They may have been by the sagacious Commission but at least one of them, potatoes, is mentioned in an exhibit at the Science Museum, South Kensington, as a source from which whisky can be obtained !

The reckless extension of the term ' whisky ' has had the gravest consequences for the prestige of the industry. It has tended to deprive whisky of the special character it had built up during centuries of careful and pious labour and research. The tasteless distillate of grain, made at one process in a patent still, is equally entitled to call itself whisky as the exquisite, pot-still, malt whisky, dried above a peat fire. It is only right to say that the definition was made in defiance of the best opinion of the distilling industry. The Duke of Richmond and Gordon, landlord of the most famous of all whisky districts, gave expression to this opinion in a speech in 1909 : ' Quite recently, a public inquiry has taken upon itself to decide, What is Whisky ? And I regret to say that apparently anything made in Scotland, whatever its combination, is to be called Scotch whisky. But for my part, I should prefer, and I think most of those whom I am addressing now would prefer, to trust their own palates rather than to the dogma of chemists.'

At the same time, it is to be deplored that the opposition of serious-minded, cultivated whisky-drinkers to the pretensions of the Whisky Commission was not stronger. It was nothing short of a sin against the light to lump malt whisky with neutral industrial spirit as if it too were something to burn in lamps, to drive engines, or to clean clothes. The evil having been done, however, it is necessary to instruct the whisky public, especially young and inexperienced drinkers, in the true facts of the case so that, so far as possible, ' whisky by grace of the Royal Commission ' may be left to those who ask for nothing more from their beverage than a ' kick '. This, at least, it will guarantee for them. But the children of light will continue

to demand of their Scotch whisky that it should
be distilled in Scotland by means of pot-stills,
from mashing materials consisting of malted
barley and nothing else, dried in kilns by peat
or other fuel according to the locality ; and of
their Irish whiskey that it should be pot-still,
from malted barley, either alone or with unmalted barley, oats, rye, or other indigenous
cereal. By accommodating themselves thus
far to modern conditions, they will assure themselves of a whisky which it will be possible to
drink without a grimace (with a heroic deter-
mination to overlook the means for the sake of
the end), and even—granted discrimination—
with delight.

The distilling of whisky is only one half of the
manufacturing process. We have still to account for the fact that though there are less
than 130 Scotch and Irish distilleries, there
are over 4000 brands of whisky on the market.
Whence comes this monstrous multiplication ?
The answer is to be found in the process known
as blending.

The practice of blending whiskies sprang up
in Scotland about 1860 as a natural development of a process which was much older,
' vatting '. By ' vatting ' is meant the mixing

of single whiskies from the same distillery but belonging to various distillations made at different periods of the year. Its purpose is to obtain a whisky of uniform character. For whisky distilled in October differs from a winter whisky and both of them differ from a spring whisky. Owing to changes in temperature, in the character of the barley, and in the chemical composition of the water employed, whisky, that master of delicate adjustments, differs from one week to another.

About 1853, spirits from the same distillery but of different ages were already being blended ; by 1865 pot-still and patent-still (*i.e.* grain) whiskies were blended for the home market. The pioneers in the revolution—for it was nothing less—were Messrs. Andrew Usher & Co. of Edinburgh whose old-vatted Glenlivet achieved a considerable reputation about that time. The practice spread and soon Glasgow, Leith, Dundee, and Aberdeen were the chief centres of a considerable blending industry. From the purely commercial point of view, blending was a tremendous benefit for the distillers. The old single malt whiskies of the Highlands were, on the whole, too powerful and heavy for sedentary town-dwellers. Blending made it possible to make a whisky which would suit different climates and different classes of patrons. For by adding the lighter Lowland malts and the neutral or almost neutral grain whiskies, in greater or less degree, a whisky could be evolved of a ' weight ' and a strength of flavour and bouquet to suit the taste or the commercial requirements of the blender. The great export trade in whisky is almost entirely due to the adaptability and elasticity which blending lent to the industry. Even to-day the aesthetics of whisky have a very definite geographical aspect. London likes a milder, less pronounced whisky than Lancashire. Lancashire in its turn affects a whisky which is lighter and less pungent in taste than that which solaces the east winds of Edinburgh. But Edinburgh is surpassed by Glasgow, where they revel in the ' denser ' and fuller-bodied joys of the Campbeltown malts. In the Highlands, malt whiskies are still drunk, uncontaminated by the diluting, chilling alliance with grain. In the country districts where the distilleries are to be found, there are devotees of the old ' single ', ' self ', or unblended whiskies. As for the export markets, Australia and India favour the lighter, drier charms of the blends *goût anglais*, in which the Highland malts have been subdued by grain and Lowland malt. But Canada, as one might have expected, tends to follow Scotland. On the continent, the Scandinavian countries display a preference for the class of whiskies which find favour in Edinburgh and its neighbourhood ; but Holland, Belgium and France, where it has become smart of recent years to ask for ' *le scotch* ', take their opinions on this important matter from the English.

The technique of blending can be briefly described. The first style may be termed the ' rough and ready '. The proportions of the different whiskies to be used are determined beforehand, in most cases upon a tried formula ; the whiskies are poured into a vat where they are mixed up thoroughly and allowed to stand for a day and a night in order that the ' marriage ' may be consummated. The blend is drawn off into casks and bottled shortly after. The result is a cheap whisky, imperfectly blended, raw and unsatisfactory in flavour. The better practice is first to prepare blends of carefully selected malt whiskies and allow these to stand in casks for about two years. When this has been done, it is a comparatively

simple matter to make a blend that will suit
an individual market. The blended malts are
run into the vat and mixed with more or less
Lowland malt and more or less grain whisky.
The resulting blend is then drawn off and left
in the cask to marry for a minimum period of
six months. The process of mixing in the vats,
which used to be done by revolving paddles,
is more usually performed in large-scale
blending by the passing of compressed air
through the mixed liquors from a large number
of small jets in the bottom of the vat. In this
manner, it is said by some, a surer and more
intimate mixture is obtained and the horrid
possibility of a subsequent failure of marriage
banished. But no technical device affects the
supreme clause in the matrimonial legislation
of whisky, that time is of the essence of the contract. Whiskies are capricious, sensitive creatures ; they are not to be flung at one another
like goats. Rather are they to be compared
to fillies which are highly likely to plant iron
heels in the belly of the too-forward stallion.
They must grow accustomed to one another
and, unless they have been carefully chosen,
no amount of time will persuade them to live
together in amity.

After the experimental stage of blending had passed, the blender evolved fairly definite rules of his craft. He no longer works in the dark ; he knows exactly what he is going to create. He begins by grading whiskies in territorial groups. Thus—to anticipate somewhat the contents of a later chapter—the whiskies of the Glenlivet district and its surrounding country (for only one whisky is legally entitled to describe itself as ' Glenlivet ', *nomen prae-clarissimum*) are ranked together ; the North Country whiskies (for the most part Aberdonian) form another class, and so on. Within certain limits the blender is aware that he can substitute one North Country whisky for another in his blend, one Speyside for another, one Islay for another. He also knows that, although there are excellent malt whiskies which would never, were they to be kept to the Judgment Day, do anything but bicker in the cask, there are unions predestined to be blessed. Thus the Banffshire whiskies can be counted upon to make a happy and enduring marriage with the Islays.

Although blenders preserve jealously the secrets of the different ingredients and their proportions in the blends, it may be taken that the whiskies which are drunk over the greater part of the world are made up from equal quantities of Highland malt whiskies and grain whiskies, with the addition of a smaller proportion of Lowland malt. Islays or Campbeltowns are also used, but they should be previously blended with the Highland malts to which they will add their own noticeable but pleasant flavours. The object of the good blender is to obtain a smoothly finished liquor in which no individual strain will thrust its characteristic taste or aroma upon the palate. The unscrupulous blender, catering for the unthinking multitude, will cheaply and rapidly obtain a whisky of sorts by adding a small quantity of a strongly flavoured Islay or Highland to a large quantity of cheap grain whisky. But the good blender (may heaven be kind to him and grant him skill !) knows that no whisky that an honest man could sell without blushing is to be got by such crude means. And here it is that the Lowland malts play their part in the scheme of things. It is their function—for they are but slightly flavoured liquids—not to add an instrument to the well-balanced orchestra, which every fine blend is, but rather to act as the conductor, giving a steadiness of rhythm

to the music. They are, as it were, catalysts ;
they act as a bridge between the pungent
Highland malts and the sexless, neutral grain
whiskies ; without their presence a fine, smooth
blend is impossible.

Blends of malt whiskies without the addition
of grain are practically unknown so far as the
ordinary public is concerned. About twenty-
five years ago, when the Highland distilleries
had large stocks in hand, an attempt was made
to create a market for blended malts. The
attempt failed, in spite of a vigorous advertising
campaign. People who had acquired a taste
for the more insipid charms of the grain-
containing blends were not to be won by the
more definite flavours, the wider range of
variations, the greater subtlety of the unblem-
ished malts. The more's the pity. Perhaps we
are not manly enough to grapple with the really
great whiskies. But some there are who have not
succumbed to the degeneracy of the age. There
is, for example, the patriarchal Professor Saintsbury who records that the best of all the blends
he has tasted was one of Clyne Lish (a Sutherland
whisky) and Smith's Glenlivet. Grain whisky
the same authority very properly describes as fit
only for drunkards and for blending.

Irish whiskies are not blended so frequently as Scotch. The best opinion is that the Irish distillations are better as ' self ' or single whiskies.

The adulteration of whisky might well have a chapter to itself—if it were not for the fact that the consumer of a reputable whisky need not fear to be its victim. Vitriol was at one time added to whisky (in very small quantities, needless to say) in order to improve the ' bead ' or bubble proof of the spirits. ' The doctor ', by which was meant a mixture of vitriol and oil of almonds, was sometimes called in by Highlanders who wished to see a froth in their casks. The same effect was artificially produced in Canadian spirits by adding glycerine and ' bead oil '. When the United States still manufactured whisky (or at least a liquid whose local name was whisky) a pleasing concoction called ' Bourbon oil ' was sometimes added to give it a frothy appearance. Bourbon oil consists of fusel oil, acetate of potassium, sulphuric acid, and other equally attractive ingredients. If such things could be done before Prohibition, one need not be surprised at anything that happens after.

IV

GEOGRAPHY

IT is fairly well known by this time (or some painstaking and persuasive authors have written in vain) that the wines of Europe are to be grouped in various more or less closely defined geographical areas. By degrees the assiduous oenophile learns to discriminate, in his infancy between Burgundy and Bordeaux, in his hobbledehoy days between, say, Mâcon and Beaujolais, and, when he reaches years of vinous discretion, he has educated his palate to the nicer expertise required to detect a Romanée Conti from a Richebourg. But who appreciates that there are geographical divisions in whisky ? Too few, it is to be feared. Yet, even as there are in the kingdom of Bordeaux fair provinces, Médoc, Graves, Sauternes, Saint-Emilion, Pomerol, for this polity of the wine is no colourless cosmopolis but, indeed, a confederation or bund, so within the ethereal realms of whisky boundaries are fixed, marking off one lordship from another ; there are territorial families in the north, at the fashion of whose marryings and giving in marriage we have already glanced. The geographical aspect of whisky is one which must receive the consideration of all who regard it as something more than a liquid whose taste, presumably offensive, one destroys with gaseous waters out of syphons.

One does not pretend that the whole explanation of whisky's divine variety is to be found in geography. In an operation so delicate and elaborate as distilling it is obvious that a considerable amount must be left to the highly-skilled technicians (artists one should rather call them) who control the mystery. But this would not account for the undoubted —though still somewhat puzzling—fact that whisky falls into well-defined classes corresponding to geographical areas. Geography exerts an influence, secret and subtle, upon whisky—and so far no one has been able to determine through what precise media it operates or to what degree each of the supposed factors is to be held responsible.

A well-informed writer in a trade publication puts the position with admirable succinctness : ' The malt distilleries . . . are surely among the most remarkable phenomena in British industry. Why a score of Highland

distilleries should produce twenty slightly different types of whisky, all good and all apparently
inimitable, no one seems to know with any
certainty.' Despairing of an adequate explanation of this along purely territorial
lines, he arrives at the conclusion that the credit
for the differences between one whisky and
another is to be attributed to the nature of the
utensils employed and to the local variations in
the method of working, variations which, being
preserved from generation to generation through
the reverent conservatism of distillers, secure
the permanence of each whisky's character.
Thus, the shape of the still in use has an
undeniable influence upon the whisky distilled
from it, for upon its shape depends the proportion of essential oils and higher alcohols
which will be collected in the condenser. And,
on the other hand, the still-man, that almost
priestly functionary, fills a rôle of the highest
importance. He has the final voice in deter-
mining the style of a whisky (within the limits
imposed upon him by his utensils and his
material) because so much depends on the
precise instant, in the course of distilling, when,
acting upon an intuition securely fortified by
experience and tradition, he stops collecting

the finished spirit and returns the remainder of the distillate to the still. Custom in manufacture, inherited and jealously guarded, necessarily plays a considerable part in bestowing traits of one kind and another upon a liquid which at the crucial moment of its birth assumes the delicate and impressionable form of a vapour. It is even held by some old distillers that a finer whisky is made if peat is used *to heat the spirit-still.* Far-fetched as it may appear, there is almost certainly something in this contention, for peat does not give such a high temperature as coal, and therefore the wash in the still is brought more gradually and steadily to the boil.

When everything has been admitted, however, in a question where the last word must remain with the chemist (always assuming that a chemist can be found capable of appreciating the more esoteric niceties of whisky's flavour and aroma, as well as of conducting experiments with test tubes and retorts) there remains the practical consideration that there *are* territorial classes of whisky. And it is not difficult to understand why there should be, even if the persistence of local distinctions in manufacture be discounted.

There are four main geographical factors brought to bear upon whisky.

First, there is air. The relative purity, humidity, etc. of the atmosphere in and around a distillery is not the least important of the character-bestowing agencies that affect whisky. Practically all the malt distilleries of Scotland are located outside large towns ; the most renowned of them stand in bare, open country, far from the smoke and the dust. The great belts of wood and heath which are characteristic of the Banffshire and Morayshire uplands cleanse the winds which sweep across them and impart some of their own purity to the whiskies of hallowed name that are distilled there. Nor is it without significance that about fifty per cent. of the Scottish distilleries stand within a few miles of the sea. There seems to be some obscure association between the qualities of sea-air and the whisky produced in it, although there is no better evidence for the opinion than the fact that a large number of distilleries flourish almost within sight of salt water.

Second, water. This is so important that it scarcely needs to be mentioned. Yet the effect of water upon the style of a whisky is negative rather than positive. Its virtue consists in adding no flavour—or at least no marked flavour—to the malt which it makes. It should be pure, colourless, without odour, free from micro-organisms or grosser organic matter, above all devoid of mineral contamination, dissolved or in suspension. Each distillery recites the praises of its water-supply. Highland Park, the well-known Orkney distillery, obtains its water from two hidden springs : ' it never sees the light from source to mash dam '. The Glen Elgin-Glenlivet distillery claims to possess (though, indeed, it is not alone in making the claim) the finest distilling water in Scotland, drawn from a mountain spring. The Glenlivet distillery relies upon ' the finest and purest water on earth, which tumbles down the mountainside for 1200 feet, and glides through the district in the sparkling stream of Livet '. The Old Bushmills distillery, one of three Irish distilleries making a pure malt spirit, employs the water of the river Bush, which flows through an extensive peat bog. There seems to be no doubt that the effect of such water upon the malt will be somewhat similar to that of the peat which the Highland distiller burns in his kiln. But, as a rule, the distilling water should conform to the specifications set out above. The purer the water the better will it perform the task of converting starch into diastase, maltose, etc., and the purer will be the subsequent vinous fermentation.

The geographical bearings of all this are obvious. Percolating through subsoil of a certain uniform character, flowing into faults in rock of a specific geological nature, and, finally, running over the stones and earth of river-beds descending from the same water-shed down the slopes of the same hills, thus does rain-water acquire a common body of local or provincial qualities. The best and the most productive whisky-district in the world is that which is served by waters flowing from the hillsides of the Cairngorms and their sister outposts of the Grampians in Banff and Moray. Let it not be assumed, however, that the same hillside will at all points yield the same water. There was once a distillery built at consider-able expense in a West Highland seaport to make use of the waters of a burn flowing from a most august mountainside. The water was all that could be wished for. It was clear and sparkling to the eye, pleasant to the palate, triumphant in the laboratory. But alas ! It had one fault. Good whisky could not be made from it. Chemists, maltsters, and still-men could try as they might : it was of no avail. The money, it seemed, had been as good as thrown away ; the glittering deceitful Highland burn had charmed thousands of pounds out of investors' pockets, for nothing. But a mile away there was another burn, this time a mere trickle of water and not particularly tempting to look at. Despair suggested an experiment with its water, which came from the same slopes as that of the deceiving burn. The result was astonishing—a whisky of high quality. It is widely used to-day in blending, and the buildings of the original distillery are now a storehouse for the new distillery that stands, a mile away, on the waters of the second burn.

Third, peat. The convenient proximity of a peat bog is an economic necessity for a High-land malt distillery. On the north shore of Scapa Flow is Hobister Moor which supplies the peat for the Highland Park distillery. The famous Faemussach Moss, with its inexhaustible peat deposits, contributes something to the distinctive flavour of Glenlivet whisky. For, of course, there is peat and peat. Good whisky is very fastidious in its tastes and demands a peat which is wholly free from mineral impregnations. Even among peats which are not contaminated in this way there is a certain amount of variety owing to differences in the vegetable composition of the fuel.

Fourth, barley. It is a little too late in the day to pretend that all whisky malts are made from barley grown in the district where the distillery is situated. It has even been said that the barley grown and ripened in a warm climate is more dependable for malting than home-grown barley, which may have suffered from rain after it was in the ' stook '. The proprietor of one well-known Speyside distillery said recently that he had examined whisky made from Californian, Danish, Australian, English and Scotch barley and had not been able to detect any very marked difference between them. Still, he confessed that, if other things were equal, he preferred to use a home-grown barley from the Scots seaboard lying between the rivers Deveron and Ness. The Glenlivet distillery has obtained its barley for generations from the same farms lying in the deep, fertile fields of the Laichs of Banff and Moray, and in this it accords with the practice of the makers of most of the classic whiskies. An inherited skill in raising barley for distillation—for a great deal depends on the degree to which the grain has been allowed to ripen before cutting, and on its garnering and threshing—accounts for the long and close association between farm and distillery which is so common in the North. And, of course, locally-grown barley, even where it is not superior to imported grain, helps to preserve the traditional character of the spirit made from it.

The whisky districts of Scotland—for Irish whiskey belongs to a separate kingdom and must receive separate notice—are four in number. They are:

1 HIGHLAND MALTS

2 ISLAY MALTS

3 CAMPBELTOWN MALTS

4 LOWLAND MALTS

The first three of these districts share in common the distinction of employing peat to dry the malt in the kiln. But the Islays and Campbeltowns are not to be thought of as mere subdivisions of the Highland area ; they are quite independent and distinct units, and the whiskies they make belong to indigenous and inimitable types which have a definite place and function in the orchestra of whisky.

There are, at the time of writing, 122 distilleries in existence in Scotland. Of these ten make Islay whiskies ; ten are in Campbeltown ; eight make Lowland malt ; one makes both grain whisky and Lowland malt ; nine produce a grain whisky ; and by far the greater number, eighty-four, distil Highland malt whisky. In other words, two-thirds of the entire whisky-distilling industry of Scotland is devoted to the manufacture of the Highland malt spirit.

The habit that distilleries have of crowding into a few closely-defined areas whose natural conditions have been proved by centuries of experience to be most suitable for distilling, is well illustrated by the Campbeltown malt whiskies. The whole of this important group of distilleries is found in or around the town of Campbeltown on the peninsula of Kintyre, which juts southward from Argyleshire to within a few miles of Northern Ireland. Within the few square miles which make up the whole of this, the smallest of the four whisky areas, a spirit is produced which differs widely from any of the other types of Scotch whiskies. The Campbeltowns are the double basses of the whisky orchestra. They are potent, full-bodied, pungent whiskies, with a flavour that is not to the liking of everyone. Indeed the market for these whiskies is largely confined to Scotland and to the western part thereof. So masterful and assertive are they that the marrying of them to obtain a smooth, evenly-matched blend is an extremely difficult business. Yet, if the full repertoire of whisky is not to be irremediably impoverished the Campbeltowns must remain. As might have been expected in an age when the standardized, anaemic grain-plus-malt are triumphant, Campbeltown distilling has been somewhat under a cloud in recent years. This district has suffered more severely than the others from trade depression. A few years ago it would have been necessary to mention seventeen Campbeltown distilleries, but in the interval the stills of seven of them have grown cold. The ten Campbeltown whiskies which remain are :

SPRINGSIDE	LOCHHEAD
RIECLACHAN	BENMORE
KINLOCH	SCOTIA
HAZELBURN (KINTYRE)	LOCHRUAN
GLENSIDE	SPRINGBANK

The Islay distilleries, also ten in number,

form a province of whisky no less autonomous and distinct than the Campbeltowns. They are sprinkled along the coast of the beautiful island of Islay off Argyleshire. We may call them the violincellos of the orchestra, somewhat less heavy and powerful of flavour than the Campbeltowns, yet perfectly equipped after their insular fashion, round and well-proportioned. More friendly and accommodating than their brothers of Kintyre, it is their glory that they make a good marriage with the Highland malts of the Spey district, bringing out the qualities of their mate without sacrificing any of their own beauties in the process. They give breadth and fullness to the harmony but they do not drown the voices of less capacious instruments. The ten Islay whiskies are :

BUNNAHABAIN	ARDBEG
CAOL ILA	MALT MILL
BRUICHLADDICH	LAPHROAIG
LOCHINDAAL	PORT ELLEN
BOWMORE	LAGAVULIN

Of these ten the most esteemed are probably Caol Ila, Ardbeg, Laphroaig, and Lagavulin, four whiskies with an almost legendary fame. The other day I met a man who during his life

as a recruit in the army was kept awake for
hours in the night by the prolonged rhapsodies
of two Highlanders, men who had nothing else
in common in the world but their affection for
and praise of Lagavulin.

On maps in histories of Scotland one often
sees a line, called the ' Highland Line ', drawn
slantingly through the country, north-east from
the Clyde estuary in Dumbartonshire through
the middle of Perthshire and then veering west
and north to include the uplands of Forfarshire, Aberdeenshire, and Morayshire. It runs
out to sea about Nairn and reappears at the
boundary of Caithness. To the west and north
of this line from the sixteenth century onwards
was the ' pale ' of the Celtic clan system and
the Gaelic speech. But the Highland Line on
a whisky map of Scotland is kinder to Celtic
susceptibilities and includes great stretches of
country which have been politically, racially,
and linguistically Lowland for long centuries.
If a straight line be drawn on the map between
Dundee on the east and Greenock in the west
it will represent the boundary between Highland and Lowland malt whiskies. Everywhere
to the north of this invisible frontier is the
dominion of the Highland whisky, its southern

outpost in Stirlingshire on the very edge of the line. (And, indeed, as in the case of other frontiers and other outposts, there is some dispute as to which territory is the rightful owner of this distillery, whose product, of less markedly Highland character than the others, appears variously as a Highland and a Lowland malt in different trade lists.)

The Highland whisky area is made up of one or two fairly distinct sub-divisions, of several scattered units which may be grouped together for convenience under county headings, and of one thronged and important core or nucleus. Ignoring this last for the moment, we shall take the Highland whiskies in rough geographical order, beginning with the most northerly.

Pomona, the main island of Orkney, forms one of the sub-divisions of the Highland area. It has three distilleries, Scapa, Stromness, and Highland Park, at Kirkwall, of which the last is probably the best known. Depending largely, as they do, on imported barley, much of which comes to them from the great grain-growing lands of the Lothians, these distilleries produce a whisky of strong individuality, resembling not the famous Banffshire makes but rather the

Aberdeenshire group of Highland malts which are sometimes given the name of ' North Country ' whiskies. Highland Park, the best of the three, is one of the small first class, the *premiers crus*, as it were, of Scotch whiskies. The distillery is the most northerly of all and one of the most ancient, having been founded in 1789 near the site of a bothy kept by one Magnus Eunson, a famous Orkney smuggler, who was beadle (*Anglicè*—verger) of the local U.P. Church and is said to have concealed his illicit spirits under the pulpit of the Church. When excisemen attended the services, not altogether for pious reasons, Eunson, we are told, used to announce the psalms in tones of exceptional unction. He was a true brother in the spirit of that other illicit but devout distiller who, in reply to the reproaches of his minister, said, ' I alloo nae sweerin' in the still, everything's dune decently and in order.' But it is unlikely that the Orkney clergy found fault with the illegal activities of their flocks. In Hall's *Travels in Scotland* (1807) we read, ' It is a shame that the clergy in the Shetland and Orkney Isles should so often wink at their churches being made depositories of smuggled goods, chiefly foreign spirits.' Indeed, if we owe the

A Map of SCOTLAND showing the Location of the Various Whisky Distilleries.

KEY TO MAP OF DISTILLERIES

1. GLEN SKIACH.
1a. FERINTOSH.
2. ORD-GLENORAN.
3. GLEN ALBYN.
4. MILLBURN.
5. GLEN MHOR.
6. BUNNAHABAIN.
7. CAOL ILA.
8. BRUICHLADDICH.
9. LOCHINDAAL.
10. BOWMORE.
11. ARDBEG.
12. MALT MILL.
13. LAPHROAIG.
14. PORT ELLEN.
15. LAGAVULIN.
16. GLENGOYNE.
17. EDRADOUR.
18. STRONACHIE.
19. GLENCOULL.
20. GLENCADAM.
21. GLENGARIOCH.
22. ARDMORE.
23. GLENCAWDOR.
24. BRACKLA.
25. DALLAS DHU.
26. BEN ROMACH.
27. GLENBURGIE.
28. MILTON-DUFF.
29. GLENLOSSIE-GLENLIVET.
30. LONGMORN-GLENLIVET.
31. LINKWOOD-GLENLIVET.
32. GLENMORAY-GLENLIVET.
33. GLENELGIN-GLENLIVET.
34. COLEBURN-GLENLIVET.
35. SPEYBURN-GLENLIVET.
36. GLENSPEY.
37. GLENROTHES-GLENLIVET.
38. GLENGRANT-GLENLIVET.
39. CRAIGELLACHIE-GLENLIVET.
40. GLENTAUCHERS-GLENLIVET.
41. INCHGOWER.
42. STRATHMILL.
43. AULTMORE-GLENLIVET.

44. STRATHISLA-MILTON KEITH.
45. KNOCKDHU.
46. BANFF.
47. MACALLAN-GLENLIVET.
48. ABERLOUR-GLENLIVET.
49. BENRINNES-GLENLIVET.
50. CONVALMORE-GLENLIVET.
51. BALVENIE-GLENLIVET.
52. TOWIEMORE-GLENLIVET.
53. PARKMORE.
54. GLENDULLAN-GLENLIVET.
55. MORTLACH.
56. GLENFIDDICH.
57. DUFFTOWN-GLENLIVET.
58. TAMDHU-GLENLIVET.
59. CARDOW.
60. IMPERIAL-GLENLIVET.
61. KNOCKANDO.
62. GLENFARCLAS-GLENLIVET.
63. DAILUAINE-GLENLIVET.
64. CRAGGANMORE-GLENLIVET.
65. BALMENACH-GLENLIVET.
66. GLENLIVET.
67. STRATHEDEN.
68. CAMERON BRIDGE.
69. AUCHTERTOOL.
70. GRANGE.
71. GLENOCHIL.
72. CAMBUS.
73. ROSEBANK.
73a. BANKIER.
74. LITTLEMILL.
75. AUCHENTOSHAN, DUNTOCHER.
76. GARTLOCH.
77. GLENKINCHIE.
78. KIRKLISTON.
79. BLADNOCH, WIGTOWN.

THE CAMPBELTOWN DISTIL-
LERIES : SPRINGSIDE, RIE-
CLACHAN, KINLOCH, HAZEL-
BURN, GLENSIDE, LOCH-
HEAD, BENMORE, SCOTIA,
LOCHRUAN, SPRINGBANK.

91

still which has given us Highland Park to the convenient blindness of the Orkney ministers, there will be those among us who will say that churches have been put to worse uses before now.

Caithness, which in the eighteenth century was sending whisky to Skye and the Hebrides, to-day furnishes one whisky, at Wick, where the Pulteney Distillery is found. Sutherland has at Brora a distillery where the famous Clyne-lish is made. This admirable malt blends exquisitely with the Speyside whiskies. We have Professor Saintsbury's word for it that the finest whisky he ever blended had for its ingredients Smith's Glenlivet and Clyne-lish. Ross-shire contributes five whiskies (Glen Skiach is not to be found in the latest register) : these are Glenmorangie, distilled at Tain, Dal-more and Teaninich from Alness on the north-ern shores of Cromarty Firth, and Ferintosh (prematurely mourned by Burns) from the other shore. In Glenoran to the north of Beauly is situated the Ord-Glenoran distillery.

Inverness-shire can scarcely be considered a natural territorial division for whisky. It con-tains several isolated distilleries or groups of distilleries whose products have no particular resemblance to one another. At each end of the Great Glen through which the Caledonian Canal passes is a small whisky district. Near Inverness are the three distilleries of Glen Albyn, Millburn, and Glen Mhor ; at Fort William, at the southern or western end of the Glen, are the distilleries of Glenlochie and Ben Nevis. But the Inverness whiskies approach the Banffshire type in character, while the Fort William products belong to a West Highland category, in which the fine Skye whisky, Talisker, is also to be remembered. The other Inverness-shire whiskies are more difficult to classify. Tomatin, made on the Findhorn, has a claim to be included in the inner ring of the Highland whiskies, the core to which reference has already been made. Dalwhinnie, styled a Strathspey whisky, is a native of the Central Highlands, born near the bank of that tributary of the Spey which drains sombre Loch Ericht ; it is more than seventy miles from the nearest of its fellow Spey whiskies.

Argyle contributes to the West Highland group Tobermory from Mull, the last of the insular whiskies, Oban, and Glenfyne, from Ardrishaig. In Perthshire there is a grouping of distilleries along the valleys of the Tay and its tributaries, the Earn and the Tummel. At Pitlochry the Blair Atholl whisky is made with, close beside it, Edradour of the poetic name ; Ballechin is distilled at Ballinluig, Aberfeldy at the charming little town of that name on the upper Tay, Glen Turret at Crieff, and Isla at Perth. All are useful, robust whiskies, somewhat below the highest grade in delicacy.

In Stirlingshire, Glengyle just scrapes into the Highland area (as the best opinion holds), and with Forfarshire we have reached the southern edge of the range of North country malts which extends to Peterhead. The beautiful glens and uplands of the Sidlaws are the cradle of Glencoull, Glencadam, and North Port, the Brechin whisky. Kincardine adds the two Mearns whiskies, Auchenblae and Glenurie, distilled at Stonehaven.

When the Aberdeenshire border is reached on the return northward journey the north country character of the malt is well-established. There are six distilleries within the county area, Lochnagar Royal at Balmoral (one of the two distilleries entitled to use the regal adjective), Strathdee in Aberdeen city, Glengarioch near Old Meldrum, Ardmore to the south of Huntly, Glenugie at Peterhead, and

Glendronach at Huntly. The last-named is probably the most distinguished of this group ; Professor Saintsbury mentions it kindly. But it seems doubtful whether a Huntly-distilled whisky should not be numbered with the Banffshire family. The county border-line is, in a case like this, of less significance than natural geographical divisions, and Huntly is situated upon a tributary of the Deveron, which rises among the Cairngorms and flows northward through the rich grain-bearing slopes that come down from the Grampians to dip into the North Sea along the east-and-west running coastline that extends from Nairn to Fraserburgh. There would be a case, then, for considering Huntly as within the same geographical area as nourishes the great Spey whiskies. We shall leave it, like Tomatin and Dalwhinnie, with a question-mark behind it.

The real heart of this whole matter of whisky lies in a rough quadrilateral of land, about fifty miles by twenty-five in area and corresponding approximately to the three Scottish counties of Nairn, Moray, and Banff. It would be no true or, at least, no very discerning lover of whisky who could enter this almost sacred zone without awe. It would be a most unimaginative man who could pass along its roads and look on its woods and fields, its pleasant hills and beautiful sea-shores without seeking for analogies in the scenery around him with the various perfections in his favourite whiskies. The tract has been very decisively marked off by nature, as if on purpose to contain and guard some hallowed mystery. To the north there is the sea, a magnificent sea, with already something in it of the Arctic chill and the Arctic eeriness. To the west is the river Nairn, to the east the Deveron. On the north, enclosing the region with a superb sculptured wall, are the two mountain masses of the Cairngorms and the Monadhliath mountains, between which the powerful Spey thrusts itself like a spear into a closing door. Five rivers water the area, passing northward (more accurately N.N.E.) to the sea : Nairn, Findhorn, Lossie, Spey and Deveron. It is one of the most fortunate areas in all Britain, in its climate, in its scene, in the fertility of its soil and the grandeur of its pine woods, in the physical dignity and mental poise of its people. Here Scandinavian, Celt, and those elder peoples who were before the Celt and seem likely to live as long as he, have met and mingled with the happiest of results. Such is the inner sanctuary, the fountain-head, the Ark of the Covenant of whisky.

Looked at from the purely quantitative aspect, this compact area has an importance which can easily be measured. Out of the 122 Scottish distilleries, eighty-four are in the Highlands ; of these eighty-four Highland distilleries forty-five are situated in this single district. Yet it must be noted at once that the names of the whisky districts as they are shown in the registers of the industry do not take cognizance of the unity of this district. Indeed it is impossible to discover any reasonable geographical basis for the district-names assumed by different distilleries, apparently by caprice. No amount of research can determine why some of these are called ' Strathspey ' whiskies and others ' Speyside '. Both are equally beside the Spey and in Strathspey. And it is not as if the names were interchangeable ; they are jealously guarded. The different trade-designations given to the whiskies belonging to this area, the central malt whiskies, are as follows : Speyside, Strathspey, Nairn, Elgin, Forres, Dufftown, Rothes, Knockando, Banffshire, Keith, Glenlivet.

The simplest and more logical sub-division of the area would be into five districts, roughly corresponding to the courses of its five principal rivers. Thus the Nairn belt would include the two whiskies at present known as Nairn whiskies ; the Findhorn belt would take in the three Forres whiskies and one of the whiskies at present grouped under Elgin ; the Lossie area would comprise the six remaining Elgin whiskies ; the Spey whiskies would number the present Strathspey and Speyside, and in addition the Rothes, Knockando, Dufftown, and Glenlivet brands, twenty-seven in all ; while the Deveron area would include those whiskies which now are called Keith and Banffshire, six. But in this matter, as in others more important, the conservatism of the distillers will probably prove unassailable.

Of the two Nairn whiskies, Royal Brackla and Glencawdor, the former is the more important. It is, in fact, one of the dozen or so best whiskies made in Scotland. In this case the barley used comes from the counties of Moray and Nairn and the water from springs high in the Cawdor Hills. It acquired the epithet ' Royal ' early in its career. In 1828 an advertisement in the *Aberdeen Chronicle* announced that Captain Fraser ' has made an arrangement to have this *much admired spirit* sent up by land, when a regular supply can be had weekly'. But by 1835, as an advertisement in *The Morning Chronicle* of London informs us, ' Brackla Highland Whisky ' had become ' Brackla, or, The King's Own Whisky '.

' His Majesty, having been pleased to distinguish this "by his Royal Command to supply his Establishment ", has placed this Whisky first on the list of British Spirits, and, when known, should in truth be termed " The Drink Divine "—only to be had of the Importers, *Graham and Co.*, New-road, facing the Mary-la-bonne workhouse.'

The whiskies at present classified as Forres brands belong to the Findhorn group I have suggested. They are three in all : Dallas Dhu, Ben Romach, Glenburgie.

Elgin, on the Lossie, gives its name to seven whiskies of which one, Milton-Duff, seems to belong by geography rather to a Findhorn group. The other six are Glenlossie-Glenlivet, Longmorn-Glenlivet, Linkwood-Glenlivet, Glenmoray-Glenlivet, Glenelgin-Glenlivet, and Coleburn-Glenlivet.

Of the whiskies belonging to the famous

Spey basin those classified as members of the Rothes district account for three, Glenspey, Glenrothes-Glenlivet, and Glengrant-Glenlivet. Dufftown includes five notable whiskies, Convalmore, Balvenie, Glendullan-Glenlivet, Mortlach, and Glenfiddich. There are twelve distilleries which own no more exact geographical title than ' Speyside '. They are Craigellachie-Glenlivet, Glentauchers-Glenlivet, Imperial-Glenlivet, Macallan-Glenlivet, Parkmore, Dufftown-Glenlivet, Daluaine-Glenlivet, Cragganmore-Glenlivet, Benrinnes-Glenlivet, Speyburn-Glenlivet, Towiemore-Glenlivet, and Glenfarclas-Glenlivet. ' Strathspey ', a designation differing from ' Speyside ' in some subtle way which no inquiry and no consultation with mere maps can elucidate, is given by three distilleries as their *pays d'origine*. In addition to Dalwhinnie, situated to the south of the Cairngorms in Badenoch and already noticed, there are Balmenach-Glenlivet and Aberlour-Glenlivet. The three Knockando whiskies are Tamdhu-Glenlivet, Cardow, and Knockando. The last-named, like the Rothes distillery, Glenspey, is owned by Messrs. W. & A. Gilbey Ltd., who use its product for the blending of their proprietary whiskies. The Banffshire malts, which may also be included in the Spey group, are Inchgower, a coastwise whisky distilled at Buckie, Banff, distilled in the county town, and Strathmill, Strathisla-Milton Keith, Knockdhu, all of which are made in or near Keith, which however is recognised as a separate district by only one whisky, Aultmore-Glenlivet.

Only one name has still to be mentioned, but it is a name of supreme importance. There is a small glen in Banffshire watered by a stream named the Livet, a tributary of the Avon which is itself a tributary of the splendid Spey. The pure waters of this mountain burn which tumble 1200 feet down the steep sides of Cairngorms do something more than drain the beautiful glen, they also form an essential ingredient in the whisky for which Glenlivet is renowned. Glenlivet has for long decades been almost a synonym for the finest of Highland whisky :

> Glenlivet it has castles three
> Drumin, Blairfindy, and Deshie,
> And also one distillery
> More famous than the castles three.

Product of a district of which a century ago it was said, ' everybody makes whisky and everyone drinks it ', Glenlivet, ' the real Glenlivet ', won an early place in the literature of whisky. Sir Walter Scott in *St. Ronan's Well*, that *locus classicus* for so much relating to the Scottish kitchen and the Scottish cellar, makes Sir Bingo treat the Captain and the Doctor to a cordial prepared in the wilds of Glenlivet. The Captain's verdict was as follows : ' By Cot, it is the only liquor fit for a gentleman to drink in the morning, if he can have the good fortune to come by it, you see.' ' Or after dinner either, Captain,' added the Doctor. ' It is worth all the wines of France for flavour, and more cordial to the system besides.' Still more eloquent and enthusiastic is the eulogy which Christopher North puts into the mouth of James Hogg, the Ettrick shepherd, and one of the most discerning of the old Scottish school of gourmets : ' Gie me the real Glenlivet, and I weel believe I could mak' drinking toddy oot o' sea water. The human mind never tires o' Glenlivet, ony mair than o' caller air. If a body could just find oot the exac' proper proportion and quantity that ought to be drunk every day, and keep to that, I verily trow that he might leeve for ever, witout dying at a', and that doctors and kirkyards would go oot o' fashion.'

In a later age, a less august authority, the

frivolous but ingenious author of *The Massacre of Macpherson*, a ditty without which no Scottish students' revel is (or was) complete, celebrated the malt in a stanza :

> Phairson had a son
> Who married Noah's daughter,
> And nearly spoilt the flood
> By trinking up ta water.
> Which he would have done—
> I, at least believe it—
> Had ta mixture been
> Only half Glenlivet.

But the most striking tribute to Smith's Glenlivet is not a literary one. There are at the present moment no fewer than twenty-six distilleries which use the name Glenlivet in a hyphenated form. These distilleries are found over an area of about three hundred square miles. There was some point in the old joke ' Glenlivet is the longest glen in Scotland ', especially since the hyphenation was not strictly observed at one time. So grave was the inconvenience to the makers of Glenlivet that in 1880 Colonel John Gordon Smith, the proprietor of the distillery, took the question to law, and it was decided that only the Glenlivet Distillery was entitled to style its product ' Glenlivet ' without qualification.

The roll of the Highland malt whiskies of
Scotland is now complete. It is an invidious
as well as difficult task to single out any for
special recommendation, yet a list of twelve
names can be made up which will probably
win all but universal acceptance as representing
Highland whisky at its most distinguished.
It is as follows : Glen Grant, Highland Park,
Glenburgie, Cardow, Balmenach, Royal
Brackla, Glenlossie, Smith's Glenlivet, Longmorn, Macallan, Linkwood, and———. But
the twelfth place I decline to fill, being
unable to decide, even after prolonged spiritual wrestling and debate, whether Talisker
or Clyne Lish should be honoured. It is a
problem which some of my readers may, in
any case, think it desirable to settle for
themselves.

The Lowland malt whiskies of Scotland are,
with one exception, distilled in a narrow belt
of country bounded on the north by the ' Highland line ' already mentioned and on the south
by a roughly parallel straight line running from
Largs on the west to St. Abb's Head on the east.
Within this area are seven distilleries, Stratheden in Fifeshire, Bankier in Stirlingshire, Rosebank at Falkirk, St. Magdalene at Linlithgow,

Glenkinchie at Haddington, Littlemill and Auchentoshan, Duntocher, both in Dumbartonshire. There is also the Yoker distillery in Glasgow making both malt and grain spirit. Far removed from this central Scottish plain, well-peppered with distilleries, is the Bladnoch distillery at Wigtown, making a whisky which, like its situation, stands somewhat apart from the rest of the Lowland malts.

The ten distilleries making a grain spirit are all to be found in the industrial Lowlands of Scotland. They are Carsebridge, Cameron Bridge, Glenochil, Port Dundas, Adelphi, Strathclyde, Yoker, Gartloch, Caledonian and North British. Glasgow and Edinburgh account for six of them. The best of these grain distillations, as established by the experience of the blenders, are Caledonian, Carsebridge, Cameron Bridge, and North British. It is maintained that these four whiskies have each a definite individuality—but this is a heresy that rouses the average malt distiller to passionate rage.

Ireland is properly considered as a separate kingdom in the world of whisky—or whiskey as we must now begin to call it. For not only has it a geographical claim to individual treatment, but there are many characteristics which mark it off from its Scottish brothers. For instance, the process of manufacture is more elaborate, there being three distinct distillations before the finished spirit is collected. For the most part it is made from a mash of barley and barley malt and not from barley malt alone, though there are some exceptions to this rule, of which old Buskmills whiskey is the most notable. Irish whiskey has somewhat fewer and less delicate varieties of flavour than Scotch (though I have known Scotsmen who preferred it to their native spirit), its range is definitely narrower, and, in the opinion of Professor Saintsbury and other authorities, it is better as a single or ' self ' whiskey than in blends. But a fine pot-still Irish whiskey is a magnificent thing indeed, even to those who are not prepared to go as far as one expert and affirm that it is possible to mistake Irish whiskey for cognac. It should be noted that the Irish variety needs more keeping than Scotch, being best after ten years or so in the cask.

There are twenty-one Irish distilleries in operation at the present time. This number, negligible when compared with the Scottish centres of manufacture, suggests strongly that Irish whiskey has failed to hold its place in the world market, and possibly that, at home, it has fought a losing battle against ' poteen ', which to-day threatens to become a source of supply for American bootleggers. In 1800 there were 124 distilleries in Ireland. It is unfortunately true that the name of Persse of Galway and other distilling firms of equal repute are no longer to be found in the semi-official trade lists, but it is still possible to find Irish whiskey in a wide enough range of makes to satisfy most tastes.

The (legal) distilling of Ireland is confined rather narrowly to a few, mostly urban, districts. Eleven distilleries (more than half of the total) are within the boundaries of Co. Down, Co. Antrim and Co. Derry in the north-east corner of the island. Of the remainder, five are in Dublin, all of them making whiskey in pot-stills. These are John Jameson's Bow Street Distillery (founded in 1780, curiously enough by a Scotsman, member of an Alloa family, and the sheriff clerk of Clackmannan), the D.W.D. or Jones Road Distillery of the Dublin Distillery company, John Power & Son's John's Lane Distillery, the Marrowbone

Lane distillery (William Jameson's) and the Thomas Street distillery (George Roe's) both of which are now owned by the Dublin Distillery Co. In the very heart of Ireland are John Locke & Co.'s Kilbeggan Distillery (Co. Westmeath) and B. Daly & Co.'s Tullamore Distillery (King's Co.). At Cork are the two distilleries of the Cork Distilleries Co. Ltd. and at Bandon, Co. Cork, Allman & Co.'s Bandon Distillery.

Of the twenty-one Irish distilleries, three make a pure malt whiskey, the famous ' Old Bushmills ' Distillery at Bushmills, Co. Antrim, near Portrush, and the Coleraine and Killowen Distilleries, both in Co. Derry. A grain spirit is distilled at Abbey Street, Londonderry, and at Avoniel and Connswater (with pot-still), Belfast. It will be seen that all these are situated in the three north-eastern counties. All the rest make a pot-still whiskey. There are two distilleries at Comber, Co. Down, both owned by the same firm, two at Londonderry, Limavady and Waterside, and one in Belfast, the Royal Irish Distillery, where Dunville's well-known whiskey is made.

Four English distilleries—three in London : Wandsworth, Hammersmith, and Three Mills ;

and one in Liverpool, Bankhall—produce grain spirit.

There is, fortunately for the reader's patience, no longer any need to discuss the geography of whisky in America (though Canadian whisky distilled from rye, maize, etc. should be mentioned as a competitor with the less distinctive Scotch blends). It may be presumed that the ingenuity of the American people is finding its own remedies for the perils of Prohibition and bootleg whisky, though, as a matter of fact, having observed the effects on the health of the population of several hard-bitten Scottish cities, of a few ' dumped ' shiploads of Kentucky rye whisky, I am inclined to doubt whether the present régime can hold much greater terrors than the old. Prohibition has added two more names to the nomenclature of whisky : ' Squirrel ' whisky, so called because it induces in its devotees an irresistible desire to climb trees, and ' Rabbit ' whisky which creates an impulse to leap and run.

But the whisky student has already enough names to remember without troubling his memory with the zoological brands of the United States. As an aid in his attempts to remember the classic whiskies, the crude

doggerel which is here appended may have
some value, although, being the work, as I
understand, of a Sassenach poetaster, it has
taken some liberties with Celtic pronunciation
which may excite the anger or derision of the
Gael.

RHYMED GUIDE

*to the Highland, Islay and Campbeltown
malt whiskies of Scotland*

Name we first the brands that rule in
Islay in the Western seas :
Bruichladdich, Lagavulin,
Bunnahabain, and Laphroaig.
Once I (lucky fellow !) fell in
With a man who had Port Ellen !
Though, indeed, as good as these
Is Bowmore or Caol Ila,
Celtic witch and arch-beguiler,
Ard Beg, Malt Mill. And I shall
Surely drink more Lochindaal.

Last port seen by westering sail,
'Twixt the tempest and the Gael,
Campbeltown in long Kintyre
Mothers there a son of fire,
Deepest-voiced of all the choir.
Solemnly we name this Hector
Of the West, this giant's nectar :
Benmore, Scotia, and Rieclachan,

GEOGRAPHY

Kinloch, Springside, Hazelburn,
Glenside, Springbank, and Lochruan,
Lochhead. Finally, to spurn
Weaklings drunk and cowards sober,
Summon we great Dalintober.

Children of the Highland hills,
Products of the Highland stills,
Now's no hour to ponder faults,
Toy with test-tubes, sniff at malts,
Open-chested must we sing :
Away with care—the drink's the thing !
Fearing neither sir nor madam,
Praise we Dufftown and Glencadam.
Wanderer over hill and moor,
Weary, welcomes Edradour,
Purchasing new strength to loin
With Glendronach or Glengoyne,
Glenlochie, or ripe Strath Dee,
Cragganmore and Benachie.
Pious priest at mass or matin,
'Mid the murmur of his Latin,
Thinks of Mortlach or Tomatin,
Sinning so, but is there any
Sin in dreaming of Balvenie,
Brackla, Millburn, or Glenfiddich,
Cardow, Banff, or Teaninich ?
Sailor after months of sailing,
Fishing, yachting, cruising, whaling,
Hears the joyous cry of ' land oh !'
Thirsts at once for choice Knockando.

Let the magistracy glower,
Let the law put forth its power,
He will drink the good Inchgower,
Tamdhu, Parkmore, Aberlour,
And damnation to the finny
Tribes of ocean in Dalwhinnie,—
Drink until the stars go out.
Not for us such deep-sea bout.
Quiet tipplers in our class
Are content with Glenfarclas,
Nor does fancy with us soar
Far beyond sound Convalmore,
Oban, Coleburn, or Dalmore,
With mayhap a straying wish
Towards Glen Elgin or Clyne Lish.
Hopeful nephew bound to see
Wealthy and repulsive aunt
(Shadows of a legacy)
Should equip him with Glen Grant,
He will find the interview
Smoother sailing on Knockdhu.
When debate grows over-heated,
Chairs thrown down and men unseated,
To restore both law and order
Bring in Dallas Dhu, Glen Cawdor,
Speyburn, Longmorn, or Strathmill.
Quick the tempest will be still
And sweet reason reign again
With the flow of Dailuaine.
If an angel unawares
Your domestic table shares,

You will not be wrong to give it
Tumblers of the real Glenlivet !
Serious poets, short of rhymes,
As we all may be betimes,—
For *ars longa, vita brevis*—
Woo the muse with good Ben Nevis,
Though the wench will come no less
For Glengarioch or Stromness,
Scapa or fine Highland Park,
Lighteners of Orcadian dark.
Men will talk most brilliant bosh
On a diet of Ferintosh,
Argue, with emphatic oaths,
Black is yellow on Glenrothes,
Prove that four and four make nine
If encouraged by Glenfyne,
And, in paradoxic fury,
Square the circle with Glenurie.
Converts have been made, they say,
To some quite grotesque belief
By Strath Isla and Glenspey
And Glenturret (made in Crieff).
Cunning preachers rope the sullen
Heathen folk in with Glendullan.
In melée or collieshangie
Glentauchers or Glenmorangie
Timid mortals will inspire
With a high heroic ire,
Though their sudden fits of wrath'll
Quickly pass before Blair Atholl.
Leaders of the hopeless charge,

Rallying for one assault more,
Should have come equipped with large
Flasks of Pulteney or of Aultmore,
Or at least another score
Liquors veterans will think good :
Isla, Ben Romach, Glen Mohr,
Balmenach, Glenburgie, Linkwood,
North Port, Angus-reared at Brechin,
Aberfeldy or Ballechin.
While the vanquished in the fray,
Fleeing to the nearest bar,
Counsel take with Auchenblae,
Comfort seek in Lochnagar,
And, when human courage fails,
Stronachie the foe assails.
Scholar, drinking with a lout,
Knocked his boon companion out,
Bawling egotistically, ' Shall an
Embecile enjoy Macallan ?
Craigellachie and Imperial
Are designed for souls aetherial ! '
Sad that academic rage
Should polute my peaceful page ;
Class and faction I abhor on
Towiemore or Ord-Glenoran ;
Ragged cap and top-hat glossy
Meet as equals on Glenlossie,
Bury hatchets in a hurry
In Glenugie or Glenmoray,
Talisker or Milton-Duff
(Damned be he cries, ' Hold, enough ! ')

GEOGRAPHY

Rounding off at last the story
(Highland section) put we Finis
With Glen Albyn, Tobermory,
Glenglassauch, and Benrinnes.

V

JUDGING, PURCHASE, AND CARE

THE EARNEST student of whisky who has learned that there exist only a hundred and twenty-two Scotch whisky distilleries and twenty-one Irish may be inclined to think that he has exhausted the subject and that it now only remains to transfer his geographical and technical knowledge to the field of practical experiment. If so, a sad disillusionment awaits him. He has left out of account the ingenuity of the blenders who, he will speedily discover, are far more important persons in the commerce of whisky than are the distillers. The measure of their power may be set down with a mathematical exactitude by reference to the current *Directory of Whisky Brands and Blends*, which reveals the astonishing fact that there are no fewer than 4044 brands of whisky (3428 Scotch, 487 Irish, and 128 — crowning horror ! — Scotch-and-Irish) which have acquired by usage an established name and proprietorship. This is what the resourceful blenders have done with the products of those hundred and forty-three distilleries ! It has to be admitted, too, that there are remarkably few signposts to guide the would-be buyer of whisky through the labyrinth of this senseless multiplication. There are hundreds of whisky-bottle labels bearing ' Finest old liqueur ', ' a blend of rare old Highland malts ', ' matured in sherry casks ', ' the finest Scotland makes ', and suchlike heartening but uninformative legends, but there are remarkably few which state what is the age of the youngest constituent in the blend, or what is the proportion of grain spirit to malt whisky, or in what distilleries the ingredient malts were made.

There seems, in fact, to be something rather like a conspiracy of silence among the proprietors of the different brands of whisky, a conspiracy to prevent the consumer from knowing what he is drinking. There are even cases where the wording of the label appears to be definitely misleading. Thus for example, it may be taken as axiomatic that no Scotch whisky bought by the bottle is a single whisky. Yet there are instances where the name of one famous distillery is prominently displayed on the label. The obvious inference is that the contents of the bottle consist entirely of the malt spirit of that one distillery—and this inference is, of course, normally without foundation. Again there is a deplorable looseness in the use of terms like ' fine liqueur whisky '. What does the expression mean ? Popularly it is supposed to indicate a whisky containing a slightly higher proportion of alcohol than usual. If this is so—and there is a wide difference of opinion in the trade on the subject—then it is no doubt a sufficient reason for the additional charge of half-a-crown or what not that the consumer is asked to pay. But it would be infinitely more satisfactory to know that the half-crown was buying not so many units of alcoholic content but an extra year or so of maturation, or a higher percentage of one or the other of the first-rank malt whiskies in the blend. After all, whisky is not firewater, and whisky-drinkers are not yet mere soakers, in spite of the scant attention paid to their enlightenment by the trade. It is not without extreme circumspection that one dares to address a few words of mild criticism and suggestion to a body of men so assured of their own commercial acumen as those who compose the whisky trade, but the present status of whisky may perhaps incline them to hearken to suggestions from a disinterested outsider.

The most urgent need of the industry would appear to be some form of trade legislation (carried out, of course, by a trade association) designed to secure a closer definition of trade terms. For example, the words ' finest old liqueur ' should not be at the mercy of any unscrupulous dealer with a job lot of grain spirit to dispose of. There ought to be a specific minimum strength and also a minimum age in the cask attached to the phrase. It might be possible, too, to establish a distinction between ' fine old liqueur ' and ' finest old liqueur '. Again, it should not be permissible to describe a brand as ' a brand of rare old Highland whiskies ' unless there is a recognised minimum proportion of Highland malt present. Leaving considerations of commercial morality aside, some such definitions seem to be recommended by expediency. The present chaotic condition of the trade is affecting the good name of whisky and is tending to array against it ever stronger forces of snobbery and contempt. The present policy of mystification only arouses the suspicion and wrath of the intelligent consumer and gives the unscrupulous proprietor an unfair advantage over his honest rivals. In the interest of the trade, as a whole, the far-sighted plan would seem to indicate a control of the trade's adjectives.

There are other matters which might be recommended, if not as suitable for internal legislation, at least as worthy the attention of individual proprietors. Thus each label on a whisky bottle ought to bear the names of the malt whiskies (grouped as Highland, Islay, Campbeltown, and Lowland) in the blend, and the exact percentage of grain spirit contained in it. In addition, it should state the number of years and months that the blend and each of its constituents has matured in cask. This will seem a somewhat drastic proposal, but the sound whiskies would only gain by it. After all, no one in his senses would dream of buying a bottle of wine if he did not have some guarantee of its age. There are, also, certain penalties attached to falsifying marks of this kind. And why should the buyer of whisky be less intent than the wine-drinker on getting a fair deal ? It is not as if age were less impor-tant in whisky than in wine. The substitution of a variety of patent metal ' caps ', stoppers, and what not for the familiar corks is a ' reform ' which in my opinion has been taken without due consideration. The cork helped to soak up the last traces of alcohols which ought to have been lost in the cask. And it was an insurance against contamination from outside. But are the new caps ?

In the meantime, while we await a change of heart—or of head—in the whisky proprietors, what are we buyers of whisky to do ? We may give up the fight and fall back on the counsel of despair which dictates the careless command ' Bottle of Scotch, please ' and trust that plenty of soda will drown the worst effects of our surrender. Or we may ask for one of the more loudly advertised concoctions, acting on the assumption that what is said in big type and said often enough cannot be false, or on the observation that, if we do not get a very good whisky thereby, we shall not get a very bad one. And there are some brands of whisky which are very bad indeed. But this policy is again something in the nature of a surrender, and, while removing us out of the range of definitely lethal whiskies, it will not take us very far along the path leading to the higher joys of usquebaugh.

A more adventurous programme, which may

involve some disappointments on the way but is certain to contain more than one delightful surprise and to have a happy ending, would begin with the happy traveller leaving the beaten track of the more-advertised brands (remember, they are intended for the great public and therefore have usually been emasculated by over-doses of grain spirit). He is now in an unmapped terrain with only his mother-wit, his nose, and his palate to guide him. The first will take him either to a wine and spirit merchant of unimpeachable repute or to one of those lesser-known brands such as Macdonald & Muir's Highland Queen, which supply some definite information as to origin, age, etc., on their labels. If he should go to a good merchant his exploration will in all probability have begun well. Let him ask for the firm's own blend ; it will surprise him what pleasure will be shown on the other side of the counter at the advent of one who does not come bustling in with a loud demand for any one of those brands that are household words. Perhaps he will be unlucky—not all wine merchants take this matter of whisky with the gravity that it deserves. But on the other hand, he may (supposing him to be in

London) come upon Justerini and Brooke's 'Club' Whisky or Hedges & Butler's 'Coronation Vat' or Chalie, Richards, Holdsworth's 'Old Matthew' or any of some scores of excellent blends. If he take the more speculative course of independent investigation among the lesser known proprietary brands, he may have the luck to hit upon one of the better whiskies such as 'Abbot's Choice' or Crawford's 'Three Star'. But even if he is not so fortunate in the beginning, he should persist. All the time he will be training his palate and discovering, if not new paradises, at any rate the adumbrations of them. For it cannot be said too often that whisky is not the uninspired humdrum thing that a visit to the average public-house would lead one to suppose.

This matter of the public-house supply of whisky is one that ought to be taken up by an organized and determined public opinion. For in most public-houses you are offered the choice of three (sometimes, with luck, four), well-known brands,—and a request for something different is apt to evoke an exhibition of that frosty and supercilious manner in which the British bar-maid excels. The adventurer who is not discouraged by these

Arctic divinities nor disheartened by one or two almost inevitable mishaps will be richly rewarded. He should get into the habit of tasting whisky, a practice which, odd as it sounds, has now quite gone out of fashion. He will find that soda-water has the effect of destroying any distinction a whisky may possess and of reducing the complex and subtle massing of flavours in a fine blend of Highland malts to the level of an ordinary grain-plus-a-little-malt combination. Let him eschew the enticing ' splash ', at least until he has put each new whisky to a severe test. Taking a small wine-glass, preferably one with a generous belly and a narrow rim, let him warm it slightly with his hand and then pour in a little of the whisky. Having assisted the process of evaporation with a gentle rocking motion of the glass, let him sniff the vapour at the rim. It should be mild and yet potent, round and ' warm ', with no trace of the objectionable acridity of raw spirit. Then he should take a sip—only a drop or two —and allow it to remain in the mouth for a few moments. There ought to be no harshness in the liquor's assault on the palate ; ' kick ' only indicates a young or badly-mannered spirit. It should be gentle, with nothing of that

' mineral ' taste about it which causes all but hardened and careless drinkers to shudder a little and contract the facial muscles ; and it ought to possess a smooth, elusive, and varied flavour in which it is difficult to distinguish a dominant constituent. Having performed this operation, the experimenter should add some water to the remainder of the spirit and drink thoughtfully ; it will be found better to use soft water for diluting, where this is possible, but it is a refinement which the beginner can spare himself.

Having satisfied himself by this simple test that he has encountered a superior whisky, the student should acquire a bottle in order, by a more prolonged association, to determine whether he and the spirit suit one another. He may, for example, find—and this will apply especially to men leading a sedentary life— that a generous content of Highland malt whiskies has the effect of making him liverish. He will then be well advised to keep the blend for special occasions, buying for ordinary use a whisky with a somewhat larger grain admixture.

The most important thing about whisky— its place of origin and malt-content apart—is its age. The student should never buy a brand whose age is not stated and guaranteed. He ought to do more, for there is no reason why he should not take a hand in improving the quality of the whisky he buys. Let him remember that, unlike wine, whisky does not ' age ' in the bottle. Even if he is buying only a few bottles at a time, he can improve a very ordinary spirit almost out of recognition if he buys one of those small sideboard casks of sherry-cask wood which cost forty shillings or thereabouts. He need not grudge the price, for it will put shillings on to the value of every bottle he drinks. As a rule the casks hold three bottles and must be refilled when they are half empty. The selective, ennobling processes of time and absorptive wood can play their part on his sideboard just as well as in the bonded warehouse, and after a few months he will begin to notice an undeniable ripening and mellowing in the whisky. This will tend to grow ever more apparent, for the older whisky will ' doctor ' the newer, smoothing out its rough corners and speeding up maturation.

There is, indeed, no reason why a man equipped with even a small cask of this kind should not make some blending experiments on his own account. He may, for example, begin by trying the effects of a mixture of a blend containing a large proportion of Highland malts with one of the common mostly-grain types. Or, growing bolder, he may write to one or two of the better-known Scottish distilleries and ask for a few bottles of a mature single whisky. My own experience is that he will usually be lucky. With a few bottles of a Speyside, an Islay, and a sound Lowland malt he will be well embarked on his career as a blender, to his own edification and the delight of his friends.

A warning should be uttered here about the age-factor in whisky. The best opinion holds that a whisky which has been more than fifteen years in the cask tends to deteriorate. It becomes ' slimy '—not in every case but frequently enough to make one treat with some degree of critical detachment the blind worship of seniority in whisky.

If the student has more time and means at his disposal than we have hitherto presumed, he may carry out his experiments on a somewhat larger scale and, in the fashion of the Scots gentry of an older day, get him a ten or fourteen gallon cask. This he should fill with a six-to-eight year-old whisky, putting a tap in half way down. When he has drunk down to the tap he will then fill once more with a potable but not too venerable spirit. He will soon find himself the happy owner of some quite unusually good whisky, even if he cannot in a day or two utter the words spoken to Professor Saintsbury by a member of an old Scottish family, ' It should be good. It comes from a hundred-gallon cask which has never been empty for a hundred years '. At the very thought of such riches and antiquity the least impressionable lover feels impelled to doff a respectful if covetous hat. A concise account of the true technique of the care of whisky was given not long ago in the will of a gentleman who left to an ' old and dear friend ' a ten-gallon cask of Scotch whisky :

' It is my desire, but without imposing any condition, that he shall from time to time, when the contents of the said cask shall reach the level of the tap now in the middle at the end of the cask, refill the said cask with five gallons of Scotch whisky, so that the said cask shall not from time to time be tilted to draw off the contents.'

I am told that it is now no use saying that there are only two correct ways to drink whisky :

neat and in small quantity as a liqueur after a
meal (but for that you must have something
better than grain spirit), or diluted with plain
water. The world asks for whisky—and soda,
and the syphon destroys the work of the still.
No more effectual way of ruining the flavour
of a good whisky could have been imagined
than this one of drowning it in a fizzing solution of carbonic acid gas. For people who like
the taste of soda-water it is no doubt an excellent combination, though one may ask, why
do they add whisky to it ? Only the other day
I heard someone who ought to have known
better say that he found whisky-and-water ' a
dead drink ' after whisky-and-soda. On the
same principle one would be entitled to describe, say, Montrachet as ' a dead drink ' after
a liaison with cheap champagne.

The Scots recognise one or two additional
methods of imbibing whisky and, as few of them
destroy the fine flavour of good malt spirit,
they may appropriately find mention here.
There is, to begin with, toddy, a potent and
stimulating compilation too often used as
medicine and too rarely as the crown and
climax of the festival. Its ingredients are simple
and few : whisky (and for this and all other

hot whisky drinks the whisky must not be the commonplace spirit of the hoardings, otherwise the fumes may be too unpleasant to be penetrated by the nose), sugar, and boiling water. The last should be poured into a tumbler until it is half full ; it should be kept there until the glass is well warmed and then poured out. Loaf-sugar (the quantity depending upon taste and past experience) should now be melted in the tumbler with a wine glassful of boiling water. It should, nay, it must, if sacred traditions are to be observed, be stirred with a silver tea-spoon. Now add a half glassful of whisky ; stir. Some more water ; another half-glass of the spirit. Stir, and serve hot.

Athole Brose is a beverage of a different character, its constituents being whisky, cold water, and heather honey, though as a matter of fact it is said to have consisted originally of oatmeal and whisky ! A formidable association ! Put a pound of honey into a bowl and dissolve it in cold water. About a teacupful of water will suffice. Stir—once more with a silver spoon—and when the water and the honey are intimately mixed add one and a half pints of whisky. You must now stir until a froth rises, upon which you bottle and keep tightly corked. On the authority of Meg Dods, the supreme arbiter of the Caledonian kitchen, ' the yolk of an egg is sometimes beat up with the brose '. This drink, which has the honour of being mentioned in *The Heart of Midlothian*, is carried into the sergeants' mess of the Argyll and Sutherland Highlanders on Hogmanay, borne by two subalterns and escorted by a piper and all the officers of the regiment. A quaich is filled for every officer and sergeant.

Other ancient whisky recipes are Auld Man's Milk, Highland Cordial, Highland Bitters, Het Pint and Caledonian Liquor. Auld Man's Milk is made by beating the yolks and whites of half a dozen eggs separately. Add to the yolks sugar and a quart of milk (or thin cream), and to this about half a pint of whisky. The whipped whites are then united with this mixture and the whole is gently stirred in a punch-bowl. Flavoured with nutmeg or lemon zest, this makes an admirable morning dram.

Highland Cordial is a somewhat more elaborate decoction whose foundation is a pint of white currants to which are added a bottle of whisky, the thin peel of a lemon, and a teaspoonful of essence of ginger. These are mixed and allowed to stand for forty-eight hours, when the liquid is strained. Then a pound of loaf sugar is added and given a day to dissolve. Now bottle and cork, and, in three months, begin to drink.

Highland Bitters is an extremely ancient beverage with a recipe somewhat difficult to assemble on short notice. First an ounce and three-quarters of gentian root and half an ounce of orange peel should be cut into small pieces and bruised in a mortar with an ounce of coriander seed, a quarter-ounce of camomile flower, half an ounce of cloves, and a quarter of an ounce of cinnamon stick. Now put in an earthenware jar and empty two bottles of whisky over it. Keep the jar air-tight for about a fortnight and then strain and bottle.

Het Pint was once—so Scottish legend runs —made with light wine and brandy. But ale and whisky have taken the place of these exotic ingredients in the beverage which was once carried (in a copper kettle) about the streets of Edinburgh and Glasgow on New Year's Morning and was also consumed on the night before a wedding and at a lying-in. A nutmeg is grated into two quarts of mild ale and brought to boiling point. To a little cold ale add some sugar and three well-beaten eggs. This is now slowly mixed with the hot ale, care being taken that the eggs do not curdle. A half pint of whisky being added, the whole is brought to boil again and then briskly poured from one vessel to another until it becomes smooth and bright.

A simpler beverage is Caledonian Liquor, which is made by dropping an ounce of oil of cinnamon on two and a half pounds of bruised loaf sugar ; a gallon of whisky—the best you can lay hands on—is added to this and, when the sugar is dissolved, the liquor is filtered and bottled.

For the serious-minded lover of whisky, however, recipes taken from antique house-hold books will have small attraction. All his time will be devoted to that romantic, un-ending quest of the true participator in the mysteries of aquavitae—the search for the perfect blend. To some men it has been vouchsafed to put lips to a glass of this legendary liquor—there was one occasion in my own life when I thought that the luck was mine—but never has a man been known to possess a bottle of the peerless distillation at the moment when he is—no, not describing its graces—but faintly adumbrating them by fantastic and far-fetched analogies, apologized for even as they are uttered. Most of us are content to believe that such a whisky exists—must exist —and to go on looking for it. One day before we die some unknown fellow traveller in a railway compartment, some Scots ghillie or Irish rustic, may produce a flask or unlabelled bottle and we shall find ourselves at last in the presence of the god himself, Dionysos Bromios, God of Whisky. And then our sensations, rewarded after years of disappointment and imperfect delight, may share the ecstasy of him who, in C. E. Montague's *Another Temple Gone*, tasted the whisky of the priestly Tom Farrell :

' Its merely material parts were, it is true, pleasant enough. They seemed while you sipped, to be honey, warm sunshine embedded in amber and topaz, the animating essence of lustrous brown velvet, and some solution of all the mellowest varnish that ever ripened for eye or ear the glow of Dutch landscape or Cremona fiddle. No sooner, however, did this probable sum of all the higher physical embodiments of geniality and ardour enter your frame than a major miracle happened in the domain of the spirit : you suddenly saw that the most freely soaring poetry, all wild graces and quick turns and abrupt calls on your wits, was just the most exact, business-like way of treating the urgent practical concerns of mankind.'